COWICHAN INDIAN SWEATERS

A Pacific Northwest Tradition

PRISCILLA A. GIBSON-ROBERTS

Photographs by John VanSant Roberts
Illustrations by Priscilla A. Gibson-Roberts

ECHO POINT BOOKS & MEDIA, LLC
Brattleboro, Vermont

Dedication
In honor of the Salish Indian knitters
of yesterday, today, and tomorrow —
may the spirit of their sweaters live forever!

Published by Echo Point Books & Media
Brattleboro, Vermont
www.EchoPointBooks.com

All rights reserved.
Neither this work nor any portions thereof may be reproduced, stored in a retrieval system, or transmitted in any capacity without written permission from the publisher.

Copyright © 1989, 1991, 2025
by Prioscilla A. Gibson-Roberts

Originally published as *Salish Indian Sweaters.*

Cowhich Indian Sweaters
ISBN: 978-1-64837-255-1 (paperback)

Edited by Karen Searle with Susan Larson-Fleming
Interior design by Patrick M. Redmond, Patrick Redmond Design, in consultation with Karen Searle of Dos Tejodoras Fiber Arts Publications.

The types are Adobe Garamond and Adobe Garamond Expert.

Cover design by Kaitlyn Whitaker

Contents

Preface   1

Introduction   3

Part I:
Salish Sweaters: Overview

CHAPTER ONE
The People and Their Textiles   5

CHAPTER TWO
The Development of the Salish Sweater   13

CHAPTER THREE
Three Profiles in Knitting   25

Part II:
Salish Sweater Yarns

CHAPTER FOUR
The Handspun Yarn   33

CHAPTER FIVE
Notes for the Handspinner   41

Part III:
Salish Sweater Techniques and Designs

CHAPTER SIX
Knitting Techniques   45

CHAPTER SEVEN
The Designs   72
Charts:
Geometric & Representational Designs   81

CHAPTER EIGHT
Notes for the Knitter   107

Bibliography   115

Index   116

Acknowledgements

This book could not have come into being without the cooperation of many people. I specifically wish to express my gratitude to those, who in their official capacity, rendered assistance to my study: Dan Savard and John Veillette of the Royal British Columbia Museum in Victoria, B.C.; Dr. Elizabeth Johnson of the University of British Columbia Museum of Anthropology in Vancouver, B.C.; Margaret Meikle, Curator of the Museum of Anthropology Cowichan Knitting Exhibit in Vancouver, B.C.; Becky Charlie of the Coqualeetza Cultural Center in Sardis, B.C.; Patricia A. John of the Sto:Lo Heritage Center in Hope, B.C.; and Betty White, a highly respected dealer in Indian arts and crafts in Cowichan Bay, B.C.

I also wish to thank the knitters who gave so much of their time, welcoming me into their homes to share their knowledge of the craft. To these I extend my undying gratitude: Nora George and Clara Charles of Westholme, B.C.; Eva Williams of Duncan, B.C.; Marge Kelly of Veddar Crossing, B.C.; and Josephine and Mike Kelly of Cultus Lake, B.C. In addition, I wish to acknowledge all unidentified knitters whose work I studied and recorded in museum collections, private collections, shops, and on the backs of friends and acquaintances across North America.

I wish to express my gratitude to my friend, Mary Sue Gee of Tacoma, Washington, for her direct assistance in collecting material and for her support and encouragement that has led me to achievements far beyond my expectations. And a special thanks to my daughter, Kimberly, whose patient editing of the text was of tremendous value and greatly appreciated. Last but not least, my heartfelt thanks to my husband, Jack, my photographer, my go-fer, my muscles, my chauffeur, the fellow who encouraged me and believed in my abilities, the fellow who gave up precious vacation time to assist me in pursuit of information, the fellow who spent countless hours in the darkroom — he truly "wore many hats," all vital to the completion of this book. My thanks to you all — I hope that my efforts are worthy of your contribution.

Priscilla A. Gibson-Roberts
October, 1988

Preface

Born in the Cowichan Band, the Salish sweater is a unique expression of the native culture and crafts. The Salish people learned how to work with a new fiber, wool, on their large handspindles to produce a heavy singles yarn. With their newly acquired knitting skills, these yarns were transformed into warm, durable garments such as socks, caps, and long underwear. They took their skills seriously, adapting the more efficient European spinning wheel to suit their desire for a heavy singles yarn similar to their spindle-spun yarns.

Through studying a knitted sweater of European origins, the Salish produced a garment suited to their needs. Not satisfied with a relatively plain garment, they incorporated designs from their former weaving skills into their sweaters. Many Scottish descendants living in this region erroneously believe that these sweaters grew out of Indian exposure to Fair Isle knitting. But a study of knitting history and working techniques of both cultures clearly indicates that these sweaters are uniquely the product of the Salish knitter. The Salish sweater evolved in the same time frame as the Fair Isle sweater. Each style is a distinct expression of its own culture.

Regretfully, the Salish, particularly the Cowichan Band in the Duncan area on Vancouver Island, have been ill-served by a system that stresses quantity over quality. To remain a viable commodity in a modern, industrialized society, handcrafted garments must be of superior quality to command a share of the market. This is no longer true of many Indian sweaters today. The problem of deteriorating quality is being further compounded by imported sweaters flooding the market. There is still a group of Salish knitters dedicated to their craft, but with this small group aging, the future looks bleak.

This book is dedicated to the goal of keeping alive the spirit of these wonderful Indian sweaters by recording their techniques and designs for future generations.

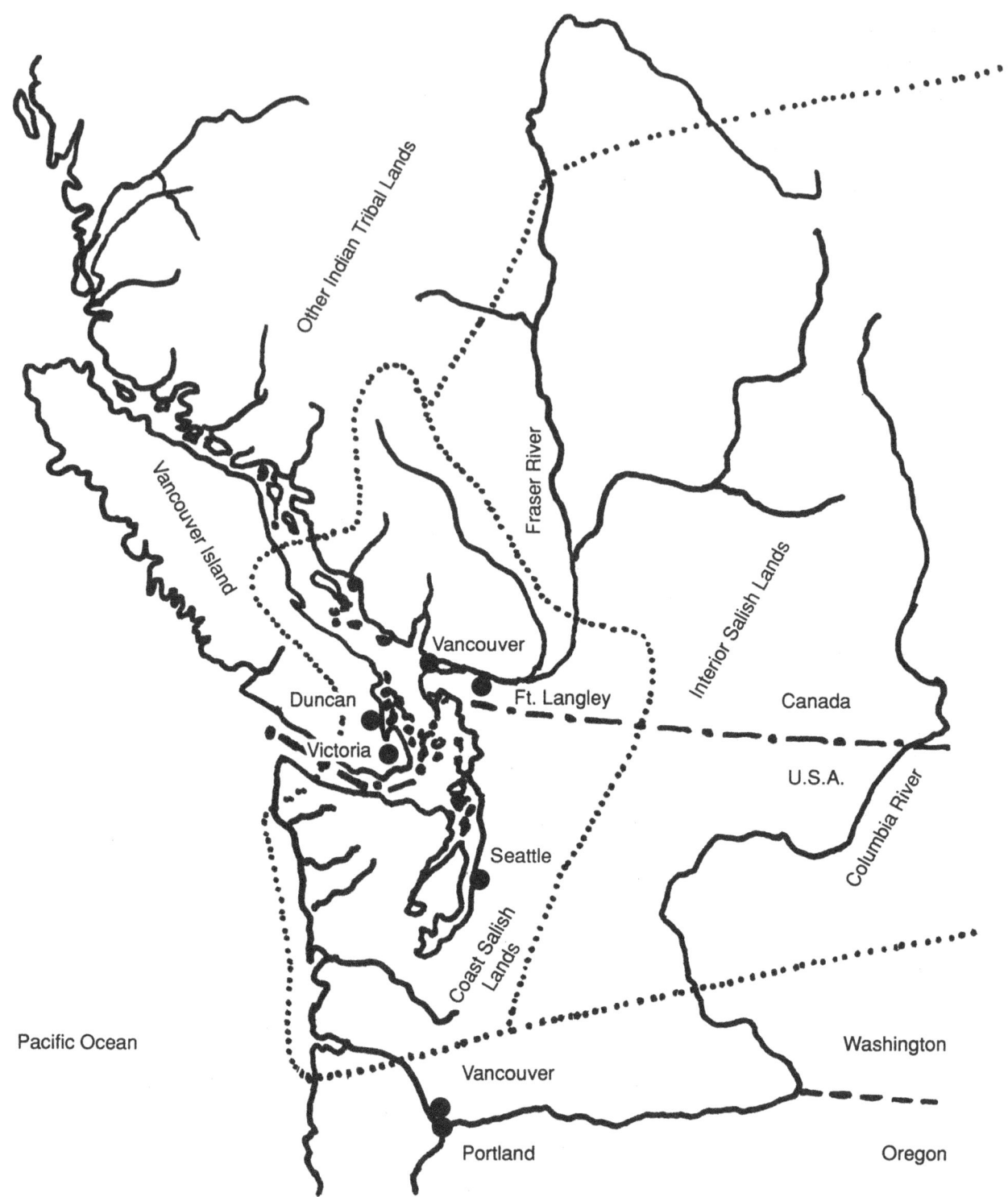

ANCESTRAL TRIBAL LANDS OF THE SALISH

INTRODUCTION

Preserving a Tradition

Every culture makes unique contributions to the arts and crafts – expressions of the people themselves, unaffected and honest. This is often reflected in the clothing preferred within the group, which, if of universal appeal, become items of commercial value. This aptly describes the Salish, or Cowichan sweaters of the Northwest.

The sweater entered the Indian world through acculturation, being a garment adapted from European immigrant culture. The Salish, having long been fiber workers, spinning and weaving blankets of goat and dog hair, quickly became knitters of considerable expertise. In the Cowichan Valley on Vancouver Island, the sweater became an expression of Salish art, coveted and collected far beyond the local environs.

My introduction to the Salish sweater, often referred to as the Cowichan sweater in deference to its origins in the Cowichan Band, a part of the Salish Tribe, was in the mid-1960s. At that time, my family resided in Washington state. It was at the Pike Street Market in Seattle, that I first saw a Salish knitter and her sweaters. And it was love at first sight! Being a

BELOW: INDIANS OF THE KOKSILAH RESERVE DISPLAYING THEIR HANDCRAFTS. NOTE THE LARGE BALL OF HANDSPUN YARN IN THE BASKET IN THE FOREGROUND AND THE BULK HEAD SPINNER MOUNTED ON A TREADLE SEWING MACHINE BASE DIRECTLY BEHIND. COURTESY OF THE GOVERNMENT OF BRITISH COLUMBIA.

knitter, I recognized the sweaters' uniqueness, and I wanted to learn more about them. Through the years I picked up bits and pieces of lore about these garments, some of it fact, some of it fiction. It was not until I began to study folk sweaters throughout the world that I realized that little had been done outside of anthropological circles to accurately record these wonderful garments

It was at this point that my current endeavor was born. I felt that the sweater itself must be recorded, not just the cultural and economic aspects of the craft. All crafts change with time, often passing into obscurity with little or nothing preserved for posterity. I did not want this to happen to this sweater; far too many special knitted garments have been lost in all parts of the world already. Knitting, being a humble craft, was not adequately revered, and as a result, many of its historic roots have withered and died without being recorded. This trend must not be allowed to continue.

I am not an anthropologist, an archaeologist, or a historian. I am a spinner and knitter, and it is from my expertise in these fields that I approached this work. Therefore, I have depended heavily upon published works in anthropology, archaeology, and history rather than upon my own independent study for materials related to the Salish culture. But the collection of material relative to the sweaters themselves comes from my own research, studying and recording stitch by stitch the techniques and designs on countless sweaters. In the process, I saw a wide range of skills demonstrated, from those disgracefully lacking in merit to those of impeccable quality. I concentrated on the latter, recording the work of master knitters of several generations, for this is the source of the enduring contributions to the craft. Many personal interviews with current knitters, most with strong family ties to the Salish knitting tradition, helped to enrich the hours spent in recording the information from the sweaters themselves. This book is the result of all those hours. Hopefully, it will help to establish the Salish Indian sweater in its rightful place in the history of knitting.

CHAPTER ONE
The People and Their Textiles

To be able to appreciate the development of the unique Salish or Cowichan sweaters, one must have some understanding of cultural and artistic development of these Northwest Coast Indian people. The Salish are not a unified tribe. They are divided into two major groups: The Coast Salish and the Interior Salish. Both language similarities and collected artifacts signify a tie between the groups, although it was only among the Coast Salish that spinning, and much later, knitting were practiced. Archaeological evidence indicates that the Coast Salish migrated from the interior to establish themselves along the lower reaches of the Fraser River, spreading north along the coast and south to encompass Puget Sound and much of the Olympic Peninsula, plus the eastern reaches of Vancouver Island. In all probability, there was a small native population already in the area when the migrations from the interior began, but it was absorbed by the larger Salish group. This would account for physical differences between the Coast Salish and the Interior Salish. As a result of their origins in the interior, the Coast Salish do not share the same cultural development as other Northwest Coast tribes as evidenced in their tools, houses, and art forms. (Ashwell, 1978; Barnett, 1955.)

To further complicate the understanding of tribal relationships, the Coast Salish themselves are not a single, cohesive group. They are divided into many smaller regional units, each with its own traditions and community spirit. These smaller units, referred to as Bands, include, among others, the Cowichan, Musqueam and Chilliwack Bands. Although separate entities, common cultural bonds have been maintained through social contacts, marriage and extended family ties within the various Bands.

The long, cold winters and short, hot summers of the interior dictated a nomadic existence in search of sustenance and protection from the elements. Moving from the interior, the Coast Salish found themselves in an area of mild climate with a great wealth of natural resources. A dependable supply of fish, small game, wild berries, bulbs and roots was available in profusion. Therefore, the nomadic

COWICHAN GIRL WRAPPED IN TRADITIONAL GOAT HAIR BLANKET, 1912. COURTESY OF THE ROYAL BRITISH COLUMBIA MUSEUM, VICTORIA, BRITISH COLUMBIA.

ways of the interior could be discarded in favor of permanently established villages. The people were able to erect substantial structures from the abundant cedar of the region, and to range from their homesites to outlying areas to collect seasonal foodstuffs. Being permanently situated allowed a social structure with rich ceremonial overtones to evolve. It also permitted the development of art forms not typically associated with the nomadic lifestyle of the interior, including the spinning of yarn and the weaving of blankets.

Basket making was practiced in almost all primitive cultures, for the need to carry and store foodstuffs was universal. Archaeological sites in the region have contained woven objects dating back at least 3000 years. At a site near Cape Flattery, a wooden box was unearthed and found to contain a folded blanket dating back some 500 years. (Gustafson, 1980.) A well-established weaving tradition existed in the 18th and 19th centuries which is recorded in the journals of early European explorers and later by traders. In many cases, these individuals collected blankets to be returned to Europe as curiosities of their adventures. There can be little doubt that Salish spinning and weaving was an indigenous art, evolving from techniques perfected in the weaving of baskets.

SALISH INDIAN WOMAN SEATED ON A TRADITIONAL BLANKET, ROTATING A LARGE HANDSPINDLE TO INSERT TWIST INTO YARN, 1915. COURTESY OF THE ROYAL BRITISH COLUMBIA MUSEUM, VICTORIA, BRITISH COLUMBIA.

Suitable fibers were in short supply for these people as they had no herds of fleece-bearing animals. The principal source of fibers was mountain goat hair collected from the shrubs and rocks during the spring molt and from pelts of goats slain for meat. The fibers were not abundant and were often supplemented with fibers from various plant sources, depending upon local availability. Some common fibers used as a filler to extend the goat hair include the fluff from fireweed, cattail and milkweed. Analysis has shown that the use of bast fibers from Indian hemp and stinging nettle were often used. In addition, some bands apparently incorporated dog hair into their yarns. Early explorers established the presence of small, Pomeranian-type dogs (later depicted in a painting completed in 1846 by Paul Kane) whose coats were shorn much like that of sheep today. This type of dog was located principally among the Salish on Vancouver Island. The dogs were apparently confined on the smaller islands offshore, for they were a source of considerable wealth. (Ashwell, 1978.) Meanwhile, on the mainland, the Chilliwack bands maintained dogs similar to the coyote with an undercoat that could be plucked for use in spinning. (Wells, 1987.)

After sufficient fibers were collected,

Early Salish Spinning

SKETCH OF SALISH TENSION RING FROM THE FRASER RIVER AREA OF BRITISH COLUMBIA, IN THE COLLECTION OF THE ROYAL BRITISH COLUMBIA MUSEUM.

SALISH INDIAN WOMAN WITH HANDSPINDLE RAISED, WINDING THE YARN ONTO A SHAFT FOR STORAGE, 1915. COURTESY OF THE ROYAL BRITISH COLUMBIA MUSEUM, VICTORIA, BRITISH COLUMBIA.

the laborious process of preparing the fiber and spinning the yarn was undertaken. First, a wooden sword-like instrument was used to beat a white clay material (diatomaceous earth) into the raw fibers to help cleanse and whiten them. The fibers were teased by hand, removing the coarse guard hairs while fluffing and aligning the fibers prior to their incorporation into a roving. The rovings were created by rolling the fibers along the thigh by hand. As the roving was extended in length by splicing on additional fibers, it could be rolled into balls preparatory to the actual spinning process.

The Salish utilized a large hand-tossed spindle common only in this region and found nowhere else in North America. The length of the spindle ranged from 36" to as much as 48" whereas the whorl diameter usually measured about 7-8". The whorl rested one-half to two-thirds of the way down the spindle. (Kissell, 1916.)

Both hands were required to rotate this unique spindle, and an external means of providing tension for elongation was provided through the use of a tension ring. This ring was suspended overhead, thereby allowing for a long stretch between ring and spindle tip. The roving was passed through the ring and attached to the spindle after first having a short section tightly twisted between the palms. The yarn created in this twisting was attached to the shaft of the spindle at the upper face of the whorl. The spinner sat on the floor, holding the spindle at an oblique angle with the butt of the spindle in the palm of the hand and the shaft supported with the other hand just below the whorl. The twist was inserted by a tossing motion of the hand supporting the shaft. Tossing to the left resulted in a Z-spun yarn while tossing to the right made an S-spun yarn. When sufficient twist was inserted into that portion between the spindle tip and tension ring, the yarn was wound onto the spindle by raising the shaft to a vertical position while rotating the spindle. Thus, more roving was drawn through the tension ring and the process repeated. (Buxton-Keenlyside, 1980; Kissell, 1916.) Studies have indicated that the singles yarns were always spun S and plied Z for the blankets. All early blankets were of a bulky two-ply yarn. (Gustafson, 1980.)

HANDCARVED SUL'SUL'TIN, OR WOODEN SPINDLE WHORL BELONGING TO NORA GEORGE, WESTHOLME, BRITISH COLUMBIA.

The Salish loom is not a true loom, for it has no heddles. The use of heddles involves a system by which groups of warp (lengthwise) yarns can be raised and lowered to separate the threads into layers, or sheds, allowing the weaver to pass weft (crosswise) yarns between the warps without further manipulation. The Salish loom is technically a fixed warp frame requiring the finger manipulation of every warp yarn in the weaving process. The construction of such a frame was simple. Two uprights with slots for crossbars were embedded in the ground. The slots were fitted with crossbars, the lower bar wedged to hold it in position at the base of the slot.

The loom was warped in one of two methods: reverse warping or tubular warping, both utilizing a continuous warp yarn. In reverse warping, a loom stick was tied to the uprights midway between the crossbars. The continuous warp yarn was attached to one end of the loom stick and then wound up and over the top crossbar, down and under the bottom crossbar, then up and over the loom stick. At this point, the direction was reversed to go down and around the bottom, then up and over the top to once again loop around the loom stick before reversing the direction once more. This process

Early Salish Weaving

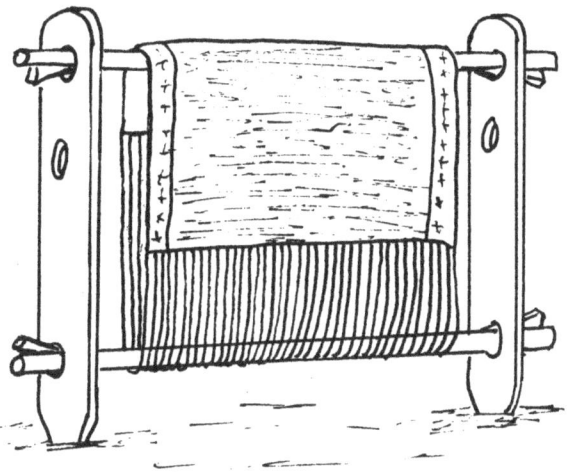

THE SALISH WEAVING LOOM, OR WEAVING FRAME EACH WARP YARN MUST BE MANIPULATED INDIVIDUALLY IN THE WEAVING PROCESS TO ALLOW FOR PASSAGE OF THE WEFT. THIS LIFTING IS VERY LABOR-INTENSIVE, A PROCESS CLOSELY RELATED TO HAND KNITTING, WHERE EACH STITCH IS CREATED AS A SINGLE ENTITY. NOTE THAT THE WEAVING BEGINS AT THE TOP OF THE LOOM AND PROGRESSES DOWNWARD.

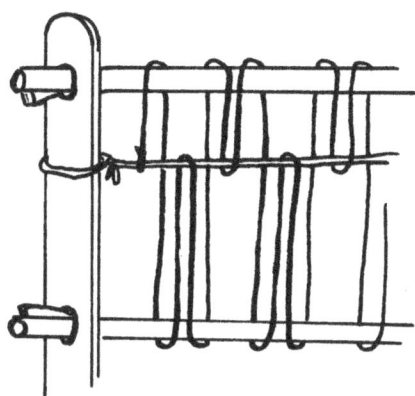

REVERSE WARPING: (ELONGATED TO SHOW THE PATH OF YARN). THIS METHOD OF WARPING ALLOWS THE CONSTRUCTION OF A FABRIC WHICH DOES NOT NEED TO BE CUT TO BE REMOVED FROM THE FRAME. A LOOM STICK OR CORD IS ADDED TO THE FRAME. THE WARP REVERSES DIRECTION AS IT PASSES AROUND THE STICK. THE STICK OR CORD IS REMOVED AFTER THE WEAVING IS COMPLETED, OPENING THE CYLINDER INTO A FLAT FABRIC.

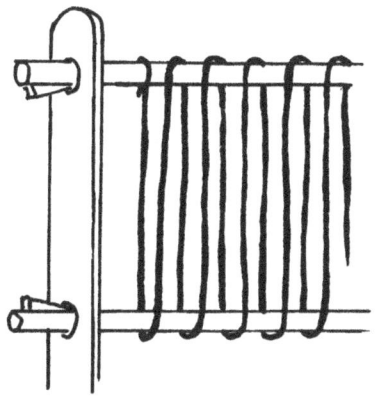

TUBULAR WARPING: (ELONGATED TO SHOW PATH OF YARN). ONE END OF THE WARP IS TIED TO THE UPPER CROSSBAR, WRAPPED AROUND AND AROUND BOTH CROSSBARS TO THE DESIRED WIDTH, THEN TIED OFF ON THE LOWER CROSSBAR. THIS METHOD REQUIRES CUTTING OF THE FABRIC TO OPEN THE CYLINDER AND REMOVE THE FLAT FABRIC FROM THE FRAME.

TWILL WEAVE: THIS DIAGONAL PATTERN IS CREATED BY WEFT FLOATS PASSING OVER TWO WARPS. AS EACH LINE IS WOVEN, THE ORDER OF CROSSING THE WARP IS ALTERED, THE WEFT FLOATS ARE STEPPED OVER ONE WARP IN EACH LINE TO CREATE THE DIAGONAL PATTERN. SALISH WEAVING TYPICALLY EMPLOYED THE COMMON TWILL OR HERRINGBONE TWILL (BELOW).

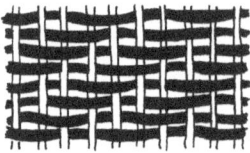 

A   B

A. COMMON TWILL: PATTERN SLANTS UPWARD IN A CONTINUAL LINE WITH A TWO-OVER, TWO-UNDER REPEAT.

B. HERRINGBONE TWILL: PATTERN SLANTS UPWARD IN ONE DIRECTION, THEN REVERSES TO SLANT IN THE OPPOSITE DIRECTION. THE REVERSAL OCCURS AT REGULAR INTERVALS.

was repeated until the desired width had been achieved. After weaving, the loom stick was removed to release the ends of the blanket.

In tubular warping, the loom stick was not used. Instead, the warp yarn was attached to one crossbar and then encircled both crossbars to the width desired. After weaving, this method required that the fabric be cut, leaving two raw edges. In both cases, the blanket length produced on this type of frame loom was twice the distance between the two crossbars.

The weaving was worked downward, necessitating an upward beat of the weft yarns. Typically, on a vertical loom, the weaving is worked upward from the bottom on the loom, thereby allowing for the easier downward beat of the weft yarns. Most Salish weavers today use the latter type.

Since there was no provision for forming a shed to control groups of warps, the weft yarns were manipulated through the warp yarns by the fingers. Short lengths of weft were used as the weaver had no shuttle with which to carry the yarn. Two variations of weaving techniques were employed, either a twill weave or a twine weave with some blankets incorporating the use of both.

The common Salish blanket, woven of handspun mountain goat hair, was largely utilitarian. The very large blankets, often ten to twelve feet long, were used for bed covers by the higher-ranking members of the various bands. The smaller blankets, five to six feet long, were used as cloaks during the cold winter months. The cloaks of lower-ranking individuals were more often woven of yarns spun from the various vegetable fibers available in the region. The common blankets were natural white in color, ornamented with simple stripes or plaids of brown or black yarn in the twill weave. (Wells, 1969.)

Ceremonial blankets, also of mountain goat hair which was often blended with dog hair, were worn as cloaks on ceremonial occasions. These often combined the simple twill and the more elaborate twined weaves; some were made entirely of twining. These blankets were ornamented with colorful bands of geometric designs at the ends and sometimes at the sides, the designs usually worked in twining. (Wells, 1969.) With the influence of European colonization and the subsequent availability of trade goods, the designs became more elaborate, combining simple geometric bands, bold central motifs and overall patterns. (Gustafson, 1980.)

The blankets were an integral part of Salish life, both practical and ceremonial. Obviously, the blanket could be used to provide warmth. But more importantly, the giving and receiving of the blanket via a potlatch determined one's social standing. The term potlatch means "to give" in the trade jargon of the area. The potlatch could be viewed as a means of sharing one's wealth, for the surplus material goods of the host were given to others with great festivity. Wealth was thus converted into prestige. The material wealth was largely measured in the accumulation of blankets. Of course, the donor could depend upon being repaid in small part for his largesse at a future potlatch given, in turn, by his guests. While only the highest-ranking members of the group staged such affairs, those of lower rank also received many gifts, causing a major redistribution of wealth.

The goat hair blankets were also important in conjunction with another ceremony, the spirit dance. This was a religious ritual of the Salish centered upon the dancer's quest for spiritual powers. At such ceremonies, the dancer called upon the spirits of his environment (animals, birds, fish, even rocks) to enter and enrich his life. An individual's success in life was bequeathed by the spirits encountered in this quest. Various articles made of spun mountain goat hair were integral to the quest, while the exchange of a goat hair blanket became a measure of personal esteem at this time. At these ceremonies, blankets were not only presented to the dancer but were often given to others in honor of the dancer.

TWINE WEAVE: WEFTS CROSS OVER AND UNDER EACH OTHER IN ADDITION TO CROSSING OVER AND UNDER THE WARPS. TWINING IS ACHIEVED ONLY BY MANIPULATING EACH INDIVIDUAL WARP. THIS WEAVE WAS OFTEN USED AT THE ENDS OF A BLANKET, WITH TWILL WEAVE COMPRISING THE BULK OF THE BLANKET. OCCASIONALLY, IT WAS USED AS A BORDER ON ALL FOUR SIDES. FEW SALISH BLANKETS WERE CONSTRUCTED ENTIRELY IN TWINE WEAVE.

The arrival of the Hudson's Bay Company was a dramatic development for the Coast Salish. With the establishment of trading posts, first at Ft. Vancouver on the Columbia River in 1826 and then at Ft. Langley on the Fraser River in 1827, inevitable changes were set into motion through contact with the white trader and

The Demise of the Salish Blanket

commercial goods. The appearance of the famous Hudson's Bay blanket irrevocably altered a way of life, with fur and salmon trade replacing the weaver's skills. (Wells, 1970.) Salmon were plentiful and could be readily exchanged for trade blankets. The native goat hair blankets were soon replaced by trade blankets, even in the great potlatches and other festivities.

With the influx of white settlers, later to be spurred by the gold rush, pressures were exerted on the Salish to discard their old traditions through governmental edict and missionary zeal. First, the traditional manner of dress, which included various degrees of undress verging on nudity, was banned. No longer could a native be seen in the white community unless dressed in a manner deemed acceptable by the Victorian code. The Indian had little choice but to adopt the white man's clothing. Next, the potlatch was outlawed by the government under the premise that participants were often impoverished after hosting the ceremony. This ritual was the very foundation of the Salish social structure. Without the ritual, the religious significance of the blanket was lost, the looms abandoned, and a way of life all but came to an end.

The final blow was dealt to the Salish way of life with the expansion of the white settlements. The Indians were forced to leave their ancestral villages and move onto reservation lands supervised by the government. No longer could they roam about their lands collecting the bountiful harvest, for that land had suddenly become private property. The Salish people were poverty stricken.

*The information contained in this chapter is based on previous publications by Ashwell, 1978; Barnett, 1955; Buxton-Keenlyside, 1980; Gustafson, 1980; Kissell, 1916; Wells, 1969 and 1987.

CHAPTER TWO

Origins of the Indian Sweater

Sheep were brought into the Puget Sound area by 1838 from both England and California. In all likelihood, flocks spread rapidly throughout the region. The Hudson's Bay Company developed farming operations in order to provide produce for their employees, and it is probable that when Ft. Victoria was established in 1843, sheep were taken to Vancouver Island. Records show that flocks were in the Cowichan Valley by 1850.

Many employees of the company and other settlers came from Scotland and its outlying islands. These people emigrated from a land steeped in textile traditions, coming from cottages that dotted a countryside where raising sheep was a major industry. Other settlers were also of British stock, from fishing villages well known for their fisherman's gansey sweaters. These people brought their European tools and skills with them, exposing the Salish to the spinning wheel and knitting needles. It was not only through the settlers that the Salish observed the use of these new tools. Mission schools were established in the area, with the Sisters of St. Ann settling at Tzouhalem in the Cowichan Valley in 1864. The curriculua of mission schools throughout the region included instruction in knitting. With their long history as fiber workers, the Salish were receptive to this new technique, for here was a craft requiring yarn manipulation reminiscent of their indigenous weaving. An outmoded craft was replaced by a new one more suited to their superimposed European lifestyle.

That the knitting skills of the Salish were of European origins is in little doubt, for there is no ethnographic or archaeological evidence to suggest indigenous roots. (Meikle, 1987.) But how the Indians learned the skills is often argued. Was it only through formal teaching or was casual contact also involved? Surely, the latter was of equal importance to formal instruction, for the Salish way of passing on skills to the young was through observation. Therefore, adults could be expected to expand their knowledge in the same way. The settlers were from the cottages and villages of Great Britain where knitting skills were passed from generation to generation. These people did not practice knitting as a parlor art, following

CHIEF GEORGE KWAKASON, KOKSILAH RESERVE, WEARING SWEATER WITH ROSE MOTIF, 1936. COURTESY OF THE ROYAL BRITISH COLUMBIA MUSEUM, VICTORIA, BRITISH COLUMBIA.

EVOLUTION OF SALISH SPINNING

COMPOSITE LINE DRAWING FROM EARLY SKETCHES BY PAUL KANE CA. 1847, PHOTOGRAPH CA. 1915, AND WRITTEN DESCRIPTIONS OF EARLY SALISH SPINDLE SPINNING.

SPINDLE SPINNING ADAPTED FOR USE WITH WOOL FIBERS AND MODERN CHAIR.

SPEED PRODUCTION OF KNITTING YARN WITH SALISH 'SPINNING MACHINE' ADAPTED BY THE INDIANS FROM EUROPEAN SPINNING TECHNOLOGY.

printed directions as did the genteel folk of the Victorian era. They mastered the craft to provide practical garments for daily living. This was folk knitting in its true form. Observed in this manner, the Salish could relate to knitting and master it readily because they were already skilled in using yarn. The techniques spread rapidly throughout the Salish bands, passing from person to person just as weaving skills had previously been passed from mother to daughter.

Most of the early knitting was limited to socks, mittens, and toques, or caps of tam styling – all items traditionally produced in tubular form on multiple double-pointed needles. Therefore, the Salish learned to knit in the round. Since they acquired their skills from people of British stock, they learned the English style of knitting: they carried their working yarn in the right hand rather than in the left in the Continental manner. As most Salish could neither read nor write, there were no written directions to follow – they simply learned the skills and knit to fit, as folk knitters throughout the world have done for generations.

The new knitting skills required them to adapt an old skill – spinning. Initially, they simply shifted to a slightly smaller spindle which more easily accommodated the new wool fibers. In doing so, the handling of the spindle was modified. Rovings were still prepared as before, but with the lighter spindle, one hand could rotate the spindle against the thigh, leaving the other hand free to draw out the roving. This system was greatly facilitated with the use of the white man's chair. In this manner, a sturdy singles yarn was produced, which, if plied, would have been cumbersome for knitting. Not only the manner of spinning was adapted, but also the type of yarn, for it was no longer a bulky two-ply yarn. Instead, a heavy-weight singles yarn was produced, spun in either an S-twist or Z-twist, the direction of twist apparently dependent upon the individual's preference.

These new skills proved to be a vital force in the survival of the Salish people. By 1900, they were in a state of social decline. They had been robbed of their lands and their culture, and decimated by disease brought in with the immigrant population. A foreign religion and lifestyle was thrust upon them, which they had little choice but to accept. The result was often extreme poverty in a land of plentiful natural resources. With their old self-sufficient ways destroyed, the men were often left unemployed, unable to compete in a new social order. Economic necessity turned the handcrafts into a cottage industry, with the women selling their traditional baskets and utilizing their new-found knitting skills to produce various articles for sale.

By the early 1900s the Salish began adding to their repertoire of knitted items by knitting knee-length underwear. This became popular not only among the native fishermen, but was also coveted by Japanese fishermen. This underwear was knit in the same manner as the socks, in the round and seamless. It remained popular through the 1930s and then disappeared from use.

At the same time, shortly after the turn of the century, a new garment was born on Vancouver Island in the Cowichan Valley. The knitters of this area, the Salish of the Cowichan Band, gave the world the now-popular Indian sweater.

THIS COMMISSIONED PULLOVER FROM ABOUT 1924 IS AN EXCELLENT EXAMPLE OF THE USE OF BLENDING TO ACHIEVE A THIRD COLOR. THE DESIGN IS WORKED IN DARK BROWN ON WHITE WITH HEATHERED BROWN AS THE MAIN COLOR. THE COLLAR DOES NOT OVERLAP AT CENTER FRONT, BUT IS REINFORCED WITH BUTTONHOLE STITCH IN MATCHING YARN IN THE AREA OF STRESS. COURTESY OF THE ROYAL BRITISH COLUMBIA MUSEUM, VICTORIA, BRITISH COLUMBIA.

Early Sweaters

The sweaters were always constructed of handspun singles yarn. Although none of the earliest Indian sweaters are known to be in existence, all of the knitters interviewed agree on its description. They were pullovers, much like the gansey sweaters, knit in the round to the underarm. The work was divided and knit to the shoulder where the join was made by binding off the front and back together. The collar was a turtleneck and the sleeves were worked from the shoulders down to the wrists. The sweater was of a single color, often with simple knit-purl designs embellishing the upper chest. At some point, a shift in style was made to a V-neck garment with a deep shawl collar and embellished with horizontal bands of color-stranded designs, still constructed in the seamless style. The actual origins of this sweater cannot be substantiated as no written record or physical evidence is available. There are two principal theories as to its evolution.

One theory, purported by many of immigrant ancestry, gives credit to Jerimina Colvin, a Scottish immigrant from the Shetland Islands who arrived in the area in 1885. It has been established that she befriended the native

SWEATER PURCHASED IN DUNCAN B.C. IN 1930, WITH DESIGN BANDS IN BLACK ON WHITE, AND GROUND IN HEATHERED GRAY. NECK HAS TWO-STITCH CENTER FRONT WITH DECREASES AT NECK EDGE; COLLAR FRONT OVERLAPS AT CENTER FRONT. SHOULDER IS WORKED IN TRIPLE BIND-OFF. COURTESY OF THE ROYAL BRITISH COLUMBIA MUSEUM, VICTORIA, BRITISH COLUMBIA.

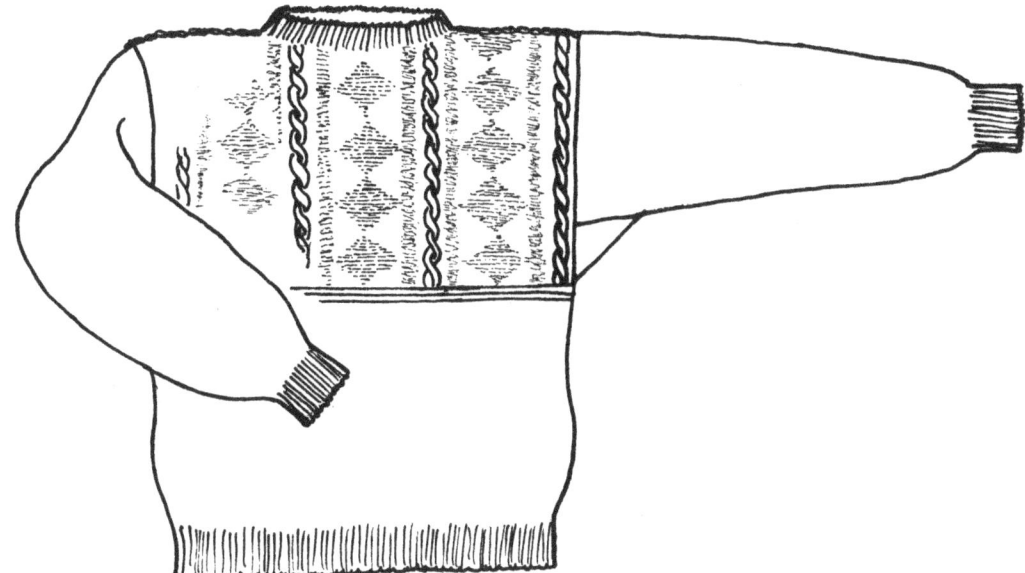

THE BRITISH FISHERMAN'S GANSEY, USUALLY KNIT IN A DURABLE 5-PLY NAVY BLUE WOOL DATES TO THE 1800S. THE HIGH-TWIST WORSTED YARN IS FIRMLY TENSIONED IN THE KNITTING. THESE SWEATERS ARE KNIT IN THE ROUND FROM LOWER EDGE TO UNDERARM, WHERE GUSSETS ARE DEVELOPED BY INCREASING. AT THE SAME TIME, SIMPLE KNIT-PURL PATTERNS AND CABLES ARE INCORPORATED AT THE UPPER BODY. WHEN THE MID-POINT OF THE GUSSET IS REACHED, THE WORK IS DIVIDED AND THE FRONT AND BACK STITCHES WORKED SEPARATELY. WHEN SHOULDER DEPTH IS REACHED, THE FRONT AND BACK STITCHES ARE BOUND OFF TOGETHER AND THE NECK FINISHED WITH A SMALL BAND. SLEEVES ARE PICKED UP AND WORKED DOWN, ALSO IN THE ROUND, TO THE WRISTBAND.

THE FAIR ISLE JERSEY IS TRADITIONALLY KNIT IN A SOFT 2-PLY SHETLAND WOOL. STRUCTURALLY BASED ON THE FISHERMAN'S GANSEY, IT DEVELOPED UNIQUE CULTURAL CHARACTERISTICS. IT IS KNIT IN THE ROUND BEGINNING WITH A LOWER EDGE RIBBING. THIS RIBBING IS OFTEN CORRUGATED, OR KNIT IN TWO COLORS, ALL KNIT STITCHES IN ONE COLOR AND ALL PURL STITCHES IN A CONTRASTING COLOR. IN THE COLOR-STRANDED HORIZONTAL PATTERN BANDS, BOTH GROUND AND DESIGN COLORS CHANGE AS THE BAND DEVELOPS. THE SMALL SYMMETRICAL PATTERNS ALLOW REGULAR USE OF EACH COLOR TO ELIMINATE LONG FLOATS. NUMEROUS PATTERNS MAY BE USED FOR THE BANDS, THE SAME ONE NEVER REPEATED ON THE BODY. GUSSETS MAY BE WORKED AT THE UNDERARM. THE WORK IS NOT DIVIDED FOR FRONT AND BACK. THE ARMHOLE IS "STEEKED" TO ALLOW THE WORK TO CONTINUE IN THE ROUND TO THE SHOULDER. THE SHOULDER IS GRAFTED, THE STEEK CUT OPEN TO THE ARMHOLE, AND SLEEVE STITCHES ARE PICKED UP TO WORK THE SLEEVE DOWN TO THE CUFF.

ORIGINS OF THE INDIAN SWEATER

SWEATER PURCHASED BY OWNER'S GRANDFATHER WHILE ON A BUSINESS TRIP, AS A GIFT FOR HIS SON, CA. 1930. DESIGN IS WORKED IN A BRASSY-BROWN YARN ON A WHITE BACKGROUND. THE GROUND COLOR BETWEEN DESIGN BANDS IS A HEATHERED YARN. THE SWEATER HAS BEEN IN ACTIVE USE SINCE ITS PURCHASE, HAVING BEEN PASSED DOWN TO ANOTHER GENERATION. COURTESY OF DEBBIE WATSON, GEORGETOWN, MASSACHUSETTS.

A 1940 ZIPPERED CARDIGAN FROM SAANICH RESERVE. NECK EDGE AND ARMHOLE ARE NOT SHAPED. THE ONLY SHAPING ON THE ENTIRE GARMENT IS A REDUCTION IN THE NUMBER OF SLEEVE STITCHES IMMEDIATELY BEFORE THE CUFF. POCKETS ARE WORKED SEPARATELY AND ATTACHED TO THE FRONTS. FROM THE COLLECTION OF THE ROYAL BRITISH COLUMBIA MUSEUM, VICTORIA, BRITISH COLUMBIA.

population, but the role she played in the development of the Salish sweater is somewhat doubtful. Mrs. Colvin emigrated from her homeland before the emergence of the color-stranded Fair Isle jersey, the supposed forerunner of the Indian sweater designs. There is no clear evidence that this type of sweater, referred to as a jersey or jumper, existed prior to the early 1900s. (Starmore, 1988.) At least one Indian sweater with color-stranded designs and shawl collar, knit on commission, has been documented to 1919. These sweaters were probably a familiar sight to the local population for the knitters to be working on commissions. This indicates that the Cowichan or Salish sweater developed in the same time frame as the Fair Isle jersey. Prior to this time, the British gansey was a traditional garment among fishermen, but color-stranded designs were limited to accessory items such as stockings, tams, and mittens. The first known sweaters produced in the early 1900s by the knitters of the Cowichan Band were of gansey styling. Jerimina Colvin's work could conceivably have been the inspiration for their early sweaters.

The true Fair Isle jersey, with color-stranded designs, exploded upon the world scene in 1922 when the Prince of Wales wore one golfing and later had his portrait painted in it. (Rutt, 1987.) Mrs. Colvin clearly worked in this genre, for she knit such a sweater in 1925 with a garter stitch collar somewhat similar to the ones favored by the indigenous knitters. This particular garment is in the collection of the Cowichan Historical Museum. It was constructed with free-floating strands on the back. Native knitters preferred to weave the stranding yarn securely onto the back surface. The relatively small garter stitch collar on Mrs. Colvin's garment was worked as a single unit. Native knitters traditionally knitted a very generous shawl collar in three units: two side fronts and the collar back, which were joined with knitting, not seamed. A true Fair Isle jersey typically had the shoulder stitches joined by grafting. Native knitters joined the pieces by binding off front and back together. Finally, the shawl collar was not of traditional Fair Isle or gansey inspiration.

A second theory is favored by the Salish knitters. Many state that the Salish acquired a sweater from a European sailor in trade on one of the smaller islands offshore, probably Valdeez Island, around 1900, and this sweater was copied by several of the Indian knitters working together. The product of their joint efforts became the prototype for the early seamless sweater of one color. None of these sweaters are known to be in existence today, and therefore cannot be studied to look for clues as to whether or not they were a self-taught adaptation. The sweaters in museum collections, dating back to 1924, are structurally related to the British gansey in that they were worked in the round, shoulders bound off together, sleeves picked up at the armhole and worked down – but without the underarm gusset of the gansey.

By this time, the sweaters had incorporated the distinctive shawl collar and woven, color-stranded designs (as is true of the 1919 sweater in private ownership mentioned earlier). The construction of the neckline, which allowed the shawl collar to conform to the body rather than shaping the garment, and the limited number of back neck stitches (only ten to twelve stitches at five to the inch to span the area) are indicative of adaptation rather than guidance by a skilled sweater maker.

The color choice and its use in the design does not resemble early Fair Isle knitting, either. In the early Cowichan sweaters, two colors were used in the design bands with the ground dividing the bands worked in a heathered yarn in natural colors. The Fair Isle jersey was very colorful, utilizing a number of colors in each horizontal band. Although only two colors were used in a single row, the designs appeared more complex than they actually were due to the constant shifting of colors through the various rows of each band of design. The popular natural-colored sweaters of the Shetland Islands did not achieve prominence until the late 1940s, long after the Indian sweaters had become a viable cottage industry.

Doubtless the basic structure of the Indian sweater had its origin in the European fisherman's sweater. It is also obvious that

FRONT AND BACK VIEWS OF EARLY PULLOVER WITH DESIGN BANDS WORKED IN GOLDEN-BRONZE ON WHITE GROUND, MAIN BODY OF GARMENT IN GRAY HEATHERED YARN. THE COLLAR HAS THE UNUSUAL TOUCH OF A LOOP BUTTONHOLE AND LEATHER BUTTON. TO ACCOMODATE GREATER FULLNESS IN THE UPPER COLLAR FRONT, STITCHES ARE PICKED UP AT THE END OF EVERY ROW ON THE NECK EDGE. ARMHOLES ARE SHAPED, A SMALL CAP WORKED ACROSS THE UPPER SLEEVES, THE KNITTING THEN CONTINUED IN THE ROUND TO THE CUFF. THIS SWEATER WAS MADE BY CHRISTINE CHARLES IN ABOUT 1950 FOR DR. HARRY HAWTHORN. IT IS THE FIRST SWEATER SHE HAD EVER KNITTED. COURTESY OF THE U.B.C. MUSEUM OF ANTHROPOLOGY, VANCOUVER, BRITISH COLUMBIA.

AT RIGHT, CHILD'S CARDIGAN WITH COLLAR IN RIBBING BY MONICA JOE, 1988. NOW IN HER MID-80S, THIS LIFE-LONG KNITTER CONCENTRATES ON CHILDREN'S SWEATERS AND ACCESSORY ITEMS, LEAVING THE LARGE, HEAVY GARMENTS TO THE YOUNGER KNITTERS. COURTESY OF BETTY WHITE'S GIFTS, COWICHAN BAY, BRITISH COLUMBIA.

ZIPPERED CARDIGAN WITH GARTER STITCH EDGING BY MARTHA GUERIN OF SONGEES, ABOUT 1966. THERE IS NO SHAPING OF EITHER NECK OR ARMHOLE, BUT THE SLEEVES ARE DECREASED IN EACH OF THE HEATHERED BANDS FOR SHAPING. COURTESY OF THE ROYAL BRITISH COLUMBIA MUSEUM, VICTORIA, BRITISH COLUMBIA.

SWEATER MADE IN THE 1970S BY NORA GEORGE FEATURING HER POPULAR BEAVER MOTIF. THE OWNER OF THE SWEATER RETURNED TO NORA IN 1986 TO HAVE THE WORN-OUT ZIPPER REPLACED. THE SWEATER ITSELF SHOWED LITTLE SIGN OF WEAR. COURTESY OF NORA GEORGE, WESTHOLME, BRITISH COLUMBIA.

many of the designs were of Scottish inspiration, and equally clear that many were inspired by Indian basketry designs. To give credit to one individual, a Scottish woman, for the sweaters seems to underestimate the ingenuity of the Cowichan knitters. Their fiber-working skills go back hundreds of years. They had been knitting for many years, possibly as early as 1860, and clearly by 1880. Knitting is a simple craft. The skills required to successfully make that first sweater were learned on the first pair of stockings completed many years before. Mrs. Colvin and other settlers were friends of native knitters. It is clearly possible that they shared their skills and inspiration for designs. But the uniqueness of several aspects of the Indian sweater (which will be clearly defined in ensuing chapters) makes them appear to be a native adaptation of a European garment, not one that was spoon-fed to the knitters by one individual. More than likely, the sweater developed from trial and error by a number of Cowichan knitters, and was later refined into a generalized structure passed from one to another and then on to the next generation.

No longer strictly a Cowichan tradition, the making of the Indian sweater spread among the Salish on Vancouver Island, eventually crossing over to the mainland bands. (Norcross, 1945.) Today, knitting such garments is practiced throughout the ancestral lands of the Coast Salish. And, although the skills used to produce these sweaters were acquired through acculturation, they are distinctly ethnic in appearance. The traditional Salish blanket had virtually disappeared. And in its place, a new tradition took root – the unique sweater evoking the traditional Indian arts of the Coast Salish.

1988 CHILD'S CARDIGAN AND CAP BY MONICA JOE. COURTESY OF BETTY WHITE'S GIFTS, COWICHAN BAY, BRITISH COLUMBIA.

Looking to the Future

The future of the Salish sweater as a cottage industry and economic force is unclear. These garments became very popular with tourists, the Japanese in particular, in the 1950s. Many traders paid one set price regardless of quality, thus encouraging new knitters to pursue the craft. With no incentive to improve, these knitters learned no more than rudimentary

MRS. PAT CHARLIE DISPLAYING ONE OF HER SWEATERS WITH A TOTEM MOTIF AND EDGING ON THE COLLAR IN TWO COLORS, 1949. COURTESY OF THE ROYAL BRITISH COLUMBIA MUSEUM, VICTORIA, BRITISH COLUMBIA.

SWEATER WITH ANOTHER VARIATION OF THE TOTEM POLE MOTIF BY MRS. PAT CHARLIE, HELD BY HER GRANDCHILDREN, 1964. COURTESY OF THE ROYAL BRITISH COLUMBIA MUSEUM, VICTORIA, BRITISH COLUMBIA.

skills. Their garments were crude imitations of the original Salish sweaters. Inferior quality proliferated and many unsuspecting consumers were subsequently disappointed with their purchases.

Because some traders made no concession for the additional time required to produce a cardigan, by far the most popular style with the consumer, many knitters made pullovers which the trader cut open to insert a zipper, thereby creating a cardigan. Cutting sweaters is a time-honored technique among folk knitters in many parts of the world, but the portion to be cut has been designed so as to leave no raw edges exposed when cut. In the case of the trader-cut cardigan, no provision was made in the knitting; rather the zipper was stitched in place and the garment simply slit open. The life of the garment was limited to the life of the zipper, for the knit stitches and the yarn tended to pull apart when attempts were made to remove and replace a worn-out zipper. Trader pressure to produce more and more garments, regardless of quality, had in many cases blackened the image of the Indian sweater. These same practices continue today. The garments are guaranteed for five years, the lifespan of the zipper. Yet the life expectancy of a well-made sweater is thirty-plus years!

Efforts have been made by many Salish leaders to control quality, but this is a cottage industry, not a unified effort whereby quality-control inspections can be enforced. These sweaters are the work of many individuals, laboring in their own homes, answering only to themselves and to market demand. Some take tremendous pride in their workmanship, spinning high quality yarns which are knit into sweaters of unsurpassed beauty. Many produce an average yarn which goes into an uninspired sweater – a mediocre product, but not a travesty considering the minimal monetary reward that the knitter will receive. Others take no pride in their craftsmanship, producing an unstable yarn loosely knit into an unwearable sweater. That such inferior sweaters are offered for sale is unthinkable, that such are purchased is unimaginable, yet both are true. As long as there is a market for inferior quality, inferior sweaters will be produced. After all, time is money to these knitters. A poorly-crafted sweater can be produced in a single day whereas a well-planned design in a well-made garment requires a week's labor. Therefore, the consumer has the final say. Until the customer is willing to pay for the labor required to produce the best quality Salish sweater, high standards of craftsmanship will not be sustained.

Salish sweaters have long been a symbol of the region, especially on Vancouver Island where they have been presented to visiting dignitaries and celebrities, and acquired hand-over-fist by tourists for generations. As with most ventures, especially handcrafting, success leads to imitation. For those knitters determined to maintain their craft, imitations have become a serious problem. The Japanese who coveted the garments are now having replicas produced in Asia and exported into North America for less money than the authentic Indian sweater. Although it is illegal to label these sweaters as Cowichan or Indian in Canada, ambiguous wording can mislead all but the most wary consumer. The competition is having a deadly effect on the future of handknitting as an economic force among the Salish.

Another more positive factor contributes to the uncertainty of this cottage

BACK VIEW OF SWEATER BY AGNES THORNE, CA. 1960. DESIGNS ARE IN BLACK ON WHITE WITH HEATHERED GROUND. SHOULDER HAS TRIPLE BIND-OFF. ARMHOLE IS SHAPED AND A SLEEVE CAP WORKED AT UPPER ARM. COURTESTY OF BETTY WHITE, COWICHAN BAY, BRITISH COLUMBIA.

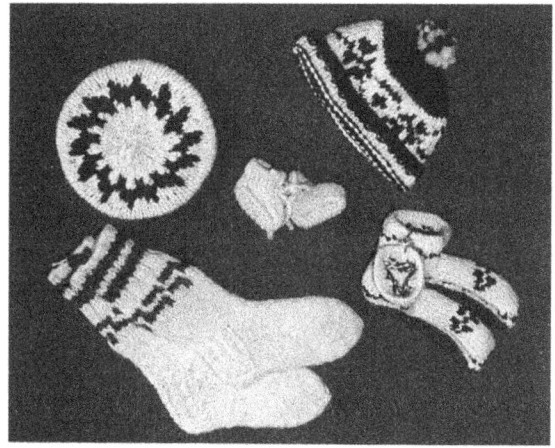

EXAMPLES OF OTHER POPULAR KNITWEAR AVAILABLE FROM THE SALISH INDIAN KNITTERS. COURTESY OF BETTY WHITE'S GIFTS, COWICHAN BAY, BRITISH COLUMBIA.

industry's future: education. Young Salish are being encouraged to stay in school to improve their educational level so that they will be more competitive in the job market of the future. This is as it should be. But it is drying up the pool of potential knitters. At best, knitting provides a subsistence or supplemental income, but it is very difficult to earn a living with handknitting. Historically throughout the world, handknitters have been faced with this problem, for the craft is exceedingly labor intensive, especially with the exclusive use of handspun yarns.

The hope for the future seems to lie in encouraging Salish youth to retain the skills for their own personal use as a matter of pride in their heritage. The Salish Indians should take great pride in their unique contribution to the world of knitting.

Note: The information in this chapter is based on publications by Ashwell, 1978; Lane, 1951; Meikle, 1987; Starmore, 1988; Wells, 1969.

AUTHOR AND FRIEND, MARY SUE GEE, LEFT, BROWSING THROUGH THE RACKS OF SWEATERS AT ONE OF MANY SHOPS OFFERING INDIAN HANDCRAFTS ON VANCOUVER ISLAND. THE UPPER AND LOWER GEOMETRIC BANDS ON THE SWEATER AT THE LEFT ARE WORKED IN A PURL-SLIP STITCH TECHNIQUE, THE ONLY TRADITIONAL TEXTURED PATTERN IN SALISH KNITTING.

Nora George of Westholme, B.C., is an artist. Given yarn and knitting needles, she creates works of art by knitting sweaters. She exemplifies the best of today's knitters, both for her skills and for her determination to keep native knitting traditions alive while also endeavoring to instill the pride of craftsmanship in the younger generation.

Nora comes from a large family of knitters, whose unique familial knitting characteristics are easily recognized: triple bind-off at shoulders, shaped armholes with a cap on

CHAPTER THREE

Three Profiles In Knitting

Nora George, Knitter

NORA GEORGE IN HER LIVING ROOM WITH THE EVER-PRESENT BASKET FILLED WITH HANDSPUN YARN AND HER LATEST CREATION. WESTHOLME, BRITISH COLUMBIA, 1986.

upper sleeves, slanted pockets, and two-color edging at the zipper, to name a few. She began to spin and knit when she was eight years old. Her mother scorned her first sweater, telling her that it was much too small to sell, but her father "put it out on the clothesline" (one method of advertising that a sweater was available to sell many years ago) and in less than a week it was sold. Nora remembers the pride she felt having sold her first sweater!

As a young woman in the 1940s, Nora was a migrant worker at a fish cannery. She was approached one day by a Japanese fisherman wanting some handknit socks. As he was willing to pay fifty cents a pair, she was determined to make him some, even though she had no tools with which to spin the yarn. She quickly improvised a spindle whorl from the lid of a five-pound lard can, added a spindle and set to work with some wool. Needless to say, she truly earned her fifty cents!

Nora remembers her mother's knitting sampler fondly. It was a long tube with all of her favorite designs which, regretfully, disappeared after her mother's death. In those days, the representational designs were simple and relatively small – swans and butterflies instead of the popular eagles and killer whales of today. The maple leaf was one of her mother's favorite designs. She simply looked at a maple leaf and worked it out with yarn, not on graph paper as knitters do today. Nora still cherishes that particular design.

In her mother's time, knitters shared designs with one another, not selfishly keeping them to themselves as many do today. Nora prefers to work in the old patterns, one of her favorites being the beaver motif shown on page 20. This particular design was acquired from a West Coast Indian, not a fellow Salish, and comes from one of their carvings. She has been using the beaver since 1956.

Life has not always been easy for Nora. She was widowed at an early age, her husband's life taken by a work-related accident. Left to raise their nine small children alone, Nora worked by day and knit by night. Her children were required to assist her, mainly by carding her wool. After the boys became skilled with the drum carder, they earned extra spending money carding wool for the neighboring spinners.

Although her children are now grown, Nora is still a very busy woman, dedicated to her family, her people, and her knitting. She longs to see all Salish knitters take pride in their craft, not to produce sweaters merely for money. She stresses quality in workmanship, based on methods used by her mother and grandmother before her. At the same time, she strives to expand her artistic abilities. The sheer beauty of her work makes it stand out from that of her peers. One of her more successful experiments has been to incorporate a third color as accent or as an outline.

Nora always takes the extra effort to make each sweater special, beginning with selecting her own wool from local producers in order to get just the qualities she is seeking. After scouring the wool, she sends it to Vancouver to be custom carded to her specifications. She then spins and knits each garment to order. Her sweaters are commissioned by people in many parts of the world, including Australia, England, and many parts of the United States, especially California.

She looks to the future with hope, both for her people and for the sweaters. She feels that to survive, her people must be proud of their heritage. Likewise, the sweaters must be of the best quality possible. She is personally involved in activities with the Cowichan Band Administration to upgrade knitting skills. She has also demonstrated and lectured about knitting at such places as the Royal British Columbia Museum in Victoria and the University of British Columbia Museum of Anthropology in Vancouver, educating consumers about the craft, so that they, too, will support good craftsmanship. Nora faces this challenge with the determination to succeed, just as she has faced living.

Betty White, Dealer and Collector

Betty White of Cowichan Bay, B.C., is a lifelong resident of Vancouver Island. Of immigrant ancestry, she is nevertheless proud of the cultural and artistic contributions of the Native American to the island's history. She is both a collector of the Northwest arts and crafts and a retailer, owning a small gift shop specializing in local art, principally that of the Indians. Obviously, Salish sweaters play an important role in her life, as they are a best seller to both residents and tourists.

Betty has also played a major role in the Indian knitting industry through the years. Among other things, she has served as a judge for the Indian knitting competition at the Duncan Fall Fair. Her major influence has been as a highly respected dealer directly involved in marketing the sweaters. In this capacity, she has been able to stress quality workmanship, both to the knitters who sell

BETTY WHITE MODELING A SWEATER KNIT BY MONICA JOE WHO STILL PRODUCES EXCELLENT GARMENTS AT 83 YEARS OF AGE. BETTY DISPLAYS A SWEATER OF MAMMOTH PROPORTIONS WEIGHING NEARLY NINE POUNDS. IT WAS KNIT ON SPECIAL ORDER BY EDITH PAGE, FREQUENT WINNER OF THE DUNCAN FAIR INDIAN KNITTING COMPETITION. COWICHAN BAY, BRITISH COLUMBIA, 1986.

through her shop, and to the consumer who buys there. Only the best knitters are represented in her shop. She is willing to pay for high-quality workmanship.

Betty has often been directly involved in determining the construction of sweaters. Among other things, all cardigans she sells must be designed as cardigans, not cut. Rather than have the zipper stitched in by machine, Betty personally inserts the zippers by hand, using heavy-duty thread and a neat backstitch. In this way, she is assured that the zipper can be replaced without damaging the sweater. She wants to see that all of the sweaters she sells live up to the life expectancy of those thirty-plus years! She also encourages the knitters that she represents to pick up the sleeve stitches at the armhole and work down to the wrist. Although she grants that a sleeve knit up and properly joined to the garment is not of inferior quality, she personally prefers the traditional method, for it allows her to easily adjust the sleeve length for the consumer!

Through the years Betty has seen many sweaters come and go – and changes in attitudes of both the knitter and the consumer. And Betty fears for the future of the Indian sweater. Most of the good knitters are getting up in years, and are not being replaced. Many new knitters are not interested in the craft itself, taking little pride in production, but instead are interested only in the money. To some extent this is understandable, since handknitting provides little more than a subsistence income.

But is it not only the passing of the older knitters that worries Betty. The older consumer who looked for good workmanship has also been replaced with a younger version whose only interest seems to be in acquiring a cheap product regardless of quality. With this double-edged sword threatening the handcrafts, she sees little hope that the art of knitting Salish sweaters will survive as a major economic force.

Josephine Kelly, Knitter and Custom Carde

Josephine Kelly of Cultus Lake, B.C., is a self-taught spinner and knitter. Her mother had been involved in the craft but died very young, so Josephine grew up without the benefit of having the skills passed down to her. She spent most of her childhood and youth in boarding school, away from the traditional family structure. It was not until her marriage to Mike Kelly that she was exposed to the traditional crafts. Using his grandmother's handmade spinning wheel, she mastered the craft of spinning. Josephine continued to use this wheel until it became worn out from years of heavy use. This spinning wheel is now a prized artifact at the Chilliwack Museum. She promptly replaced this spinning wheel, and has worn out more than one since!

An avid handcrafter, Josephine has been in a favored position. She has always had

JOSEPHINE KELLY DISPLAYING ONE OF HER SWEATERS. HER HANDSPUN YARN IS IN THE CHAIR AND A TRADITIONAL SALISH WEAVING IS ON CHAIR BACK. CULTUS LAKE, BRITISH COLUMBIA, 1988.

financial security, for her husband was employed continuously in the logging industry before his retirement. Having seven children to raise, the pursuit of spinning and knitting provided a supplemental income and some luxuries for her large family. Living on the mainland, she was not exposed to the pressures to produce exerted by many of the dealers on Vancouver Island, nor to the island's intense competition among knitters. For her, knitting has been a way of life, not a matter of life itself.

Through the years, Josephine has been actively involved in advancing the handcrafts of the tribe. In this capacity, she demonstrated spinning and knitting for many years at the Hudson's Bay Company, in museums in Vancouver, and at the British Columbia Native Craft Show.

She has been actively involved in both the sweater aspect of Indian handcrafts, and also in the revival of Salish weaving led by the late Oliver Wells. It was due to her involvement with bringing back the weaving traditions that she became a custom carder. At first she provided handspun yarns for the looms. When more of her people became involved in this activity, she recognized the need for a dependable supply of prepared fibers from the local wools to supply the spinning wheels. She approaches her role as a custom carder as a service to her people, and is looking forward to passing on the operation to someone else, so she can spend more time at her knitting. She uses much of her income to collect Salish weavings.

Josephine has a very realistic view of the future of the Salish sweater. She is of the opinion that as a traditional garment, the Indian sweater is here to stay – but not necessarily as a cottage industry on a large scale. The young are no longer interested in pursuing the craft with an eye toward sales. Rather, those who are practicing the art are presently doing so for their own use.

CLEAN WOOL HUNG OUT TO DRY ON CLOTHESLINE
INDICATES THAT A SPINER-KNITTER LIVES WITHIN.
NEAR DUNCAN, BRITISH COLUMBIA, 1986.

An integral part of any sweater is the yarn from which it is knit. The yarn determines the visual character and physical properties of the garment. In the Salish sweater, a woolen handspun singles yarn is used exclusively for knitting. This is a major contributing factor to the unique character of the garment.

Although some Indians kept small flocks for their own use and still do so today, the Salish as a group were not shepherds. They depended upon local farmers within their region to supply the fleece. From the start, the natives indicated a strong preference for the natural-colored wools. Normally, a colored fleece is considered inferior to commercial wool buyers seeking clean white wool for the mills. White fleece garners a higher price on the open market, and breeders typically cull the colored lambs for eventual slaughter. But with a ready market at hand among the Salish, breeders in this region began to develop colored flocks to meet the local demand.

Historically, all of the knitters worked with local wools. Today's knitter has several options: (1) She can obtain the fleece from a local farmer and prepare the wool herself, in the

CHAPTER FOUR

The Handspun Yarn

The Wool and Its Preparation

SPINNING WHEELS FROM TWO CULTURES. THE SMALL UPRIGHT SPINNING WHEEL AT LEFT IS DESIGNED FOR THE FINE YARNS TYPICAL OF THE EUROPEAN CULTURE; THIS ONE IS A MODERN VERSION OF THE STYLE FREQUENTLY USED ON THE SHETLAND ISLANDS. THE SPINNING WHEEL ON THE RIGHT IS DESIGNED FOR THE BULKY YARNS OF THE SALISH INDIANS; THIS ONE IS A VERSION MADE BY A NON-INDIAN CRAFTSMAN.

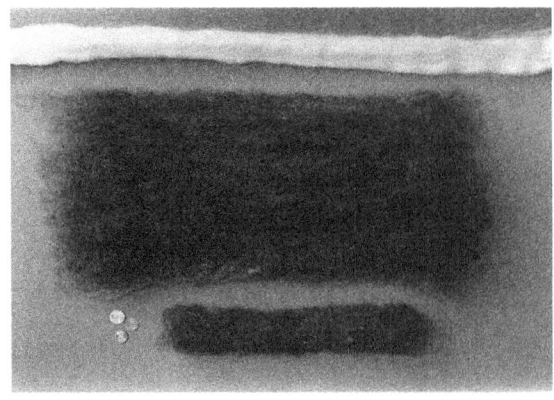

WOOL FIBERS CAN BE PACKAGED FOR SPINNING IN SEVERAL WAYS. AT TOP IS A COMMERCIAL ROVING READY FOR SPINNING. BELOW IS A HANDCARDED ROLAG READY FOR SPINNING. IN THE CENTER IS A WOOL BATT FROM A DRUM CARDER, USED FOR SPINNING BULKY YARNS. IT WILL BE TORN INTO FOUR LENGTHWISE SECTIONS. THE COINS AT LOWER LEFT ARE A REFERENCE FOR RELATIVE SIZE.

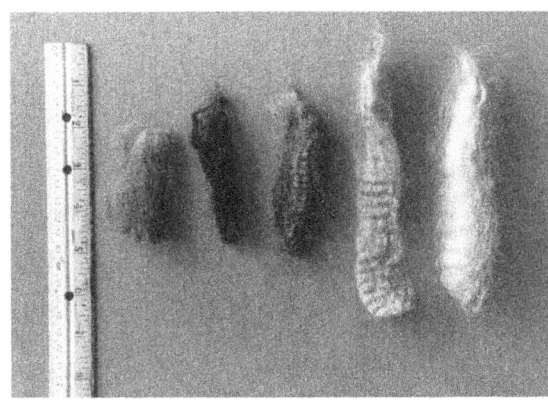

WOOL STAPLES OF VARIOUS LEVELS OF CRIMP AND LENGTH, BEGINNING AT LEFT WITH A SHORT DOWN WOOL WITH FINE CRIMP, TWO SAMPLES WITH MEDIUM LENGTH CRIMP, AND TWO SAMPLES OF LONGER-FIBER LUSTROUS WOOLS WITH OPEN, WAVY CRIMP.

traditional manner. (2) She can obtain the fleece locally, scour the wool to clean it, and then send it out to a custom carder to be prepared for spinning. (3) She can obtain a commercially-prepared roving that is ready to spin, often an imported wool from New Zealand or Mexico. Many of the sweater dealers with major retail outlets supply roving to the knitters in trade for a part of the purchase price of the garment. The final option, using commercial rovings, offers greater speed to the knitter, but is more costly and the knitter loses control over the character of the yarn. The first option, whereby the knitter does all the preparation, offers the greatest control over both character and color, but is very labor intensive. The better knitters tend to compromise by selecting their own fleece locally and then have it custom carded to save processing time.

The knitters who purchase the fleece – which they all refer to as "local wool" – do not appear to prefer one particular breed over another. Most simply select the wool to suit their needs, choosing from what is readily available from neighboring farmers. First, they look at the color and then at the characteristics of the fiber itself. Many jealously guard the identity of their supplier, fearing competition for a particularly fine colored fleece. But the knitters do not agree on what constitutes a "good" color, even with white wools. Some prefer a pure white while others look for "yellow wool." All knitters seem to prefer a staple length of about four inches, because shorter fibers will not make a sturdy bulky-weight singles yarn, and longer fibers are more difficult to card. Some like to find wools with an open, wavy crimp, some luster and a silky hand, stating that these wools make a sturdier yarn, therefore a more durable sweater. Others look for a finer, more tightly crimped wool with a soft hand, for these spin into softer, more lofty yarns; hence the sweater will be somewhat lighter in weight, yet exceedingly warm. But, within reason, they basically take what they can find. (It should be pointed out that there are breeders in the United States catering to handspinners, who offer "Salish wool" for sale. This is not a breed in the sense of the Navajo sheep and is in no way connected with the Salish Indians.)

Research has shown that early knitters often dyed the wool for their sweaters. The earliest dyes were obtained from vegetal dyestuffs which produced a golden-brown tone that appears natural to the untrained eye. The source of this color was often the berries of the Oregon grape holly combined with the bark from the balsam tree. Packaged dyes were also used after they became readily available, but were also mixed to produce a color that would have the appearance of a natural colored wool. Whether the earliest sweaters were made of dyed wools or of natural colored wools is unclear. In time, when sufficient colored wools were available, dyeing was abandoned and only the natural colored fleece was utilized.

In the first step of wool preparation, the fleece is skirted, and all the undesirable portions discarded. All good, usable wool will then be blended in order to ensure sufficient quantity to spin the desired yarns. Sorting a fleece first to separate each section according to fiber characteristics (length, crimp, color, etc.) is not usually done by most Salish spinners.

The next step in preparing the raw fleece for spinning is to remove the dirt and excess grease through scouring. Scouring is not a harsh treatment, but rather a gentle soak in warm water with a mild detergent. After this cleansing soak, the wool is rinsed and excess moisture extracted. The wool is hung on the clothesline or fence to dry. In the spring and early summer, the home of a spinner-knitter can often be readily spotted! (See photo, page 32.) None of the knitters appear to work with grease wool, that is, wool that has not been scoured. After scouring, the knitter can pass the wool on to the custom carder, indicating how it is to be prepared and blended.

If the knitter is preparing her own wool, the next step is teasing. The wool is opened and fluffed, and extraneous matter is removed. Prior to the acquisition of hand carders, early Indian knitters spun their yarns directly from the teased fiber.

After teasing, the wool is ready to be carded. Carding is a process by which the locks of fibers are fully opened and put into general

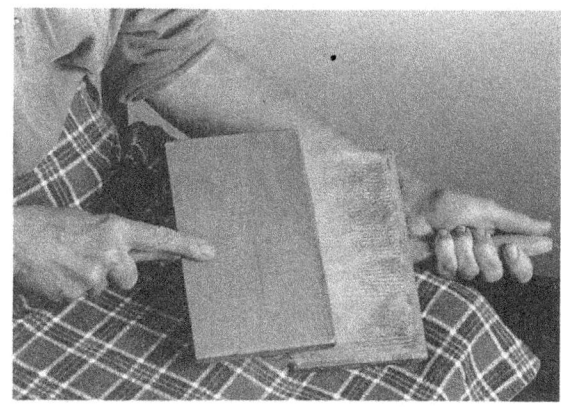

CARDING WOOL WITH SET OF HAND CARDERS

CARDER ON TOP IS DRAWN OVER THE LOWER CARDER TO OPEN AND ALIGN THE FIBERS PRIOR TO SPINNING.

THE HANDSPUN YARN

alignment. This can be achieved with either hand carders or a drum carder. Hand carders were common among the Salish from about 1890 to 1930, but were replaced with the more efficient drum carder by about 1930. Even then, hand carders continued in part-time use until about 1950, for the Indians often performed migrant labor during part of the year and the more portable hand carders allowed the knitter to carry her work along.

Hand carding was a laborious process, often assigned to the children. Hand carders are simply a pair of rectangular pieces of wood with handles attached to the backs. A carding cloth is mounted on the face of the rectangles. This cloth is made of leather or a vulcanized material with many wire hooks. The teased wool is loaded onto the face of one carder and then brushed with the other carder. The wool is transferred from one to the other in this manner, the process repeated as often as

JOSEPHINE KELLY CARDING WOOL ON SMALL-SCALE COMMERCIAL EQUIPMENT. CUSTOM CARDING OPERATIONS SUCH AS THIS ALLOW THE SPINNER-KNITTERS TO SELECT LOCAL WOOL AND HAVE IT CARDED TO THEIR SPECIFICATIONS. CULTUS LAKE, BRITISH COLUMBIA, 1986.

necessary to prepare the wool to the spinner's satisfaction. The wool fibers are then gently removed from the face of the carder and rolled into a long tube called a rolag. The wool is then ready for spinning, but as the yarn for the Indian sweater is quite bulky, many rolags are necessary before spinning can begin.

The hand carder was replaced with the drum carder, beginning in the 1930s, greatly increasing an individual's production. The drum carder consists of two rollers mounted in a frame. Both cylindrical rollers are covered with the same carding cloth used on hand carders. The larger roller, the drum, is rotated clockwise by means of a handle. A drive mechanism attached to this large roller rotates the smaller roller counterclockwise in turn. The teased wool is placed on a feed pan which leads into the small roller, called the licker. The licker picks up the wool and passes it onto the drum, straightening the fibers in the process. This process is continued until the cloth on the drum is loaded with wool. The wool is then lifted off of the drum as the handle is turned backwards. Well-prepared wool has been put through the drum carder two or three times. The resulting rectangular mass of fibers is called a *batt* and is ready for spinning. Few Indian knitters use drum carders today and the hand carders have been virtually abandoned.

By 1970, most knitters were sending their wool to custom carding operations for preparation. Today, commercial roving is in common use. Although much more costly, it allows for greater production. The more particular knitters prefer to work with a custom carder for they feel they can maintain some control over the color blending and be assured of getting the wool characteristics they deem most important.

Changes in wool preparation methods through the years have altered the appearance of the sweaters. The first color-stranded sweaters were knit in three colors: white, a natural-colored wool, and a heathered color. This heathered color can only be achieved during fiber preparation, for it consists of the white and colored wool blended together in the carding process. Most knitters today who incorporate the third color are truly using a

CARDING WOOL WITH DRUM CARDER. TEASED WOOL IS PLACED ON THE FEED TRAY TO BE PICKED UP ON THE SMALLER ROLLER (LICKER) AND TRANSFERRED TO THE LARGER ROLLER (DRUM) TO OPEN AND ALIGN FIBERS PRIOR TO SPINNING.

THE HANDSPUN YARN

The Indian Head Spinner

third color – a white, a light colored wool, and a dark colored wool. This drastically alters the unified color scheme that can only be achieved through blending the wools. Therefore, many knitters choose to use only two colors.

Historically, the first knitting yarns were spun on the traditional Salish spindle. But the preferred tool was a "spinning machine," a tool which greatly increased the speed of producing yarn. The first Salish spinning wheels date into the 1890s.

The Salish were exposed to the European spinning wheel with the arrival of the Scottish settlers. These spinning wheels were designed to produce the fine yarns normally used by the immigrant. With their narrow orifice and small bobbins, they would not accommodate the thick yarns of the Salish tradition. It was obvious that such equipment could increase native yarn production tremendously, and this bit of European technology was quickly adapted to suit their particular needs. At first, the Salish used abandoned treadle sewing machines for the base of their spinners. In place of the sewing machine head, they created a bobbin and flyer of proportions suitable for their traditional bulky yarns. The resulting spinning wheel was bobbin lead, the treadle wheel directly powering the bobbin, with a brake on the flyer. It was characterized by its strong draw, allowing for the spinning of a bulky yarn with relatively low twist. This new style of spinning wheel was of gigantic proportions compared to the typical European spinning wheel.

In using this new style of spinning wheel, the spinner did not face the orifice, but was required to position her body at an angle to accommodate the drawing action to the left. Therefore, some of the Salish refined their spinning wheels, putting the bulk head atop a homemade base with the wheel at the rear, allowing the spinner to sit facing the orifice. Today, most of the treadle-power wheels have been abandoned in favor of electric motors to power the spinning head.

This adaptation of the spinning wheel was very successful, and success breeds

EARLY SALISH SPINNING HEAD MADE OF WOOD AND PIPE. OF MASSIVE PROPORTIONS, THIS TYPE OF SPINNING HEAD WAS DESIGNED TO BE MOUNTED ON A TREADLE SEWING MACHINE BASE. COURTESY OF THE ROYAL BRITISH COLUMBIA MUSEUM, VICTORIA, BRITISH COLUMBIA.

imitators. The Indian spinning wheel was copied by many non-Indian craftsmen with the advent of a spinning revival in the late 1960s in the United States, Canada, New Zealand, and Great Britain. Often referred to as a *bulk head spinner*, sometimes as an *Indian head spinner*, few people using these spinning wheels today are aware of their origins in the Salish knitting tradition.

The yarn used in the Salish sweaters is a *woolen* yarn, meaning that it is spun from carded fibers (as opposed to a *worsted* yarn, spun from combed fibers). The early yarns were big, heavyweight yarns, heavier than a four-ply knitting worsted weight but worked to a similar gauge as the four-ply yarn. These yarns were firmly twisted singles yarns, spun both S and Z according to individual preference, and knit to a gauge of 4 to 5 stitches to the inch. The angle of twist typically measured about 30-35° while their thickness ranged from 6 to 8 wraps per inch. In the 1960s, a much bulkier yarn became popular, knit to a gauge of 2.5-3 stitches to the inch with the yarns spun at a 20-25° angle of twist and a thickness of 4 to 5 wraps per inch. The latter yarn is a bit more lofty and softer than the former yarn, yet still of durable high quality. Today's yarns all appear to be spun Z.

Note: All yarn measurements were taken on finished yarn under no tension. In the case of older pieces, measurements were taken where the garment was in need of repair, thus allowing a small portion of the yarn to be studied.

Setting The Twist

After spinning, the yarn is wound into skeins and thoroughly wetted, usually in warm water. The excess water is extracted and the skein hung to dry. In some cases, the spinner prefers to block the yarn for a week or ten days prior to wetting, helping to set the twist in advance. Others prefer to set the twist in very hot water. Regardless of the method, the twist is always set with moisture. None of the spinners appear to weight or block the wet yarn, not wanting to compromise its loft.

After the twist is set, the yarn is rolled into huge balls, often weighing as much as two

The Yarn

TWO SUITABLE YARNS: THE BULKY, SOFTLY-SPUN YARN OF GREATER DIAMETER IN POPULAR USE TODAY, (ABOVE) AND ONE OF THE FINER-DIAMETER AND HIGHER-TWIST YARNS USED IN EARLIER SWEATERS.

WRAPS PER INCH: A METHOD OF MEASURING RELATIVE DIAMETER OF ANY GIVEN YARN. MORE WRAPS ARE REQUIRED TO WRAP AROUND A ONE-INCH LENGTH WITH FINER THE YARN; FEWER WRAPS FOR HEAVIER YARN. IN THIS SAMPLE, 2" OF THE RULER HAS BEEN WRAPPED EIGHT TIMES AROUND; THEREFORE THE YARN MEASURES 4 WRAPS PER INCH.

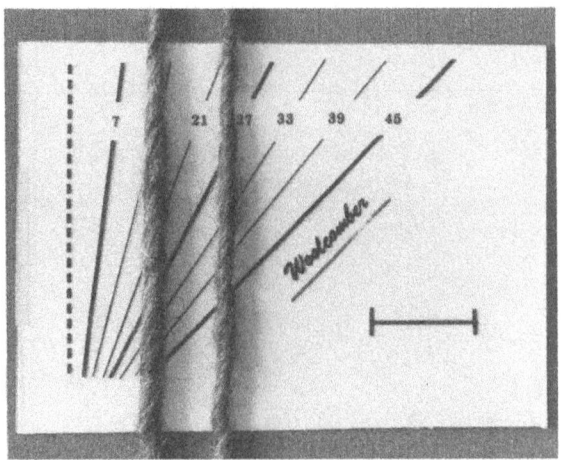

ANGLE OF TWIST: MEASURES RELATIVE LEVEL OF TWIST IN THE YARN, AN INDICATOR OF THE AMOUNT OF TWIST INSERTED INTO THE YARN. TO MEASURE THE TWIST ANGLE, LINE THE YARN UP WITH THE VERTICAL DOTTED LINE ON THE MEASURE. THEN MOVE THE YARN TO THE RIGHT UNTIL THE ANGLE OF TWIST IN THE YARN LINES UP WITH ONE OF THE ANGLE LINES. THIS INDICATES THE ANGLE OF TWIST FOR THAT PARTICULAR SECTION OF YARN. THE YARN ON THE LEFT MEASURES APPROXIMATELY 21° WHILE THE YARN ON THE RIGHT MEASURES APPROXIMATELY 33.°

pounds. During the knitting, the yarn is never knotted to join in a new strand. Rather, the yarn is frayed out for a short distance at the end and spliced with the new strand, also frayed out. In the splicing, the yarns are rolled together between the palms to help hold them together.

Note: Historical information in this chapter is based on the previously published works by Buxton-Keenlyside, 1980; Kissell 1916; and Lane, 1951.

CHAPTER FIVE
Notes for the Handspinner

Equipment

Spinning a good quality bulky yarn is not an easy task for most handspinners. This is not always due to lack of skill, although considerable skill is required. The type of equipment used is more important than skill in this case. Most handspinners have spinning wheels of traditional European design, which are suitable for finer yarns.

To produce bulky yarns on a regular basis requires a spinning wheel with a low wheel-to-whorl ratio (10:1 or less), large orfice and hooks, plus a large-capacity bobbin. These factors alone are not sufficient to ensure ease in spinning a bulky singles yarn. The system for powering the drive wheel is also a critical factor. The most suitable mechanism is a single drive belt, a bobbin lead and a brake of flyer design. This type of spinning wheel has tremendous "take-in" capacity. The draw of the bobbin on the yarn is intense, the single most important factor in producing a good bulky knitting yarn.

For the spinner who does not plan to produce bulky yarns on a regular basis, a large hand spindle is the tool of choice. This is an inexpensive alternative to acquiring a wheel. The skills required for producing a good yarn on the handspindle are relatively easy to master.

Fleece

The next factor to consider is the choice of fleece. Most medium wools and many of the finer grades of coarser wools will serve adequately for spinning bulky yarns. A wool with finer crimp will produce a lofty yarn of relatively light weight. However, the fine wools are shorter in staple length, and thus are not as suitable for bulky yarns, since shorter fibers require more twist to hold them together. The long-staple wools make a very durable bulky yarn, but their more open crimp produces a heavier yarn. (The weights can be lessened to some degree by minimizing the level of twist.) A good, uniform medium wool with a 3 to 5 inch staple and good crimp is most desirable. The fleece from the Columbia, Corriedale, Finnsheep, Oxford and Cheviot breeds are all suitable, along with most Dorsett, Romney and Perendale fleece.

Spinning a bulky, lofty yarn requires a large quantity of wool. For this reason, sorting a fleece should not be necessary. The fleece selected should be uniform, the whole fleece sharing similar fiber characteristics, so that the need for sorting is minimal. The fleece should be carefully blended in the teasing/carding process, thereby creating a uniform fiber mix.

Fiber Preparation

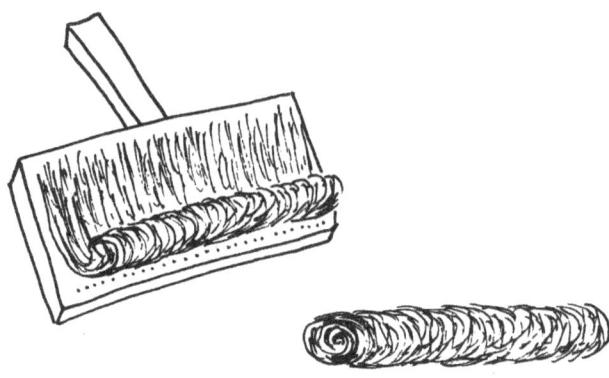

HANDCARDER AND ROLAG

THE FIBERS ARE LIFTED FROM THE CARD SURFACE AND ROLLED INTO A CYLINDER. SPINNING FROM A ROLAG RESULTS IN A LOFTY YARN.

Ease of spinning and control over yarn size and twist depend on a well-prepared fiber supply. The quality of the carding is critical, for the yarn can be no better than the quality of the fiber supply. Combing is not a desireable preparation process for Salish-type yarns, as the resulting yarn is too dense and heavy for the proposed end use.

A drum carder with an oversized drum is best for handling the sheer volume of fleece necessary for producing bulky yarns. The carder is also an excellent tool for blending. First, tease the wool, then card it into batts. Stack the batts and divide them into sections. Each section must contain a portion of the original batt from the first carding. Re-card the sections into new batts and repeat the process at least once more. Blending in this manner ensures a uniform fiber supply even though the fleece was not sorted. Blending is the method for obtaining a good color mix in heathered yarns.

Prior to spinning, tear the batts into lengthwise strips of a size appropriate for the volume of yarn to be produced. The batts from most drum carders can be divided into four sections. Divide the batts in half, gently pulling apart the fibers from the middle of the batt outward. Repeat this process on the resulting portions. Try to keep the strips uniform for this will ease the spinning of a uniform yarn.

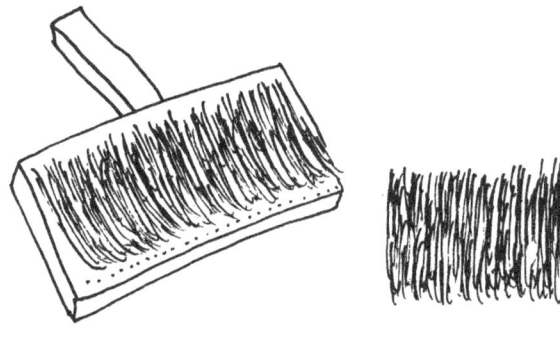

HANDCARDED BATT

THE FIBERS ARE LIFTED FROM THE CARD SURFACE AND LEFT IN A FLAT SHEET.

Spinning

Even experienced spinners will find their first efforts with an Indian-head spinner to be daunting. To reduce the level of frustration, remove all tension from the brake. Braking is seldom necessary until the bobbin is two-thirds full. Slow treadling is important. Rapid treadling inserts too much twist.

Practice a short draw in the beginning. Keep one hand at the orfice controlling the flow of twist while holding the fiber supply with the other. The hand at the orifice does not draw the fibers out of the supply, it merely controls the flow of twist and adds tension for the other hand to draw against. Draw the hand with the fiber supply back, releasing fibers in sufficient quantity for the yarn. Move this hand forward to allow the yarn to wind onto the bobbin. With practice, the length of the draw can be extended for greater speed. Regardless of the length of the draw, the hand holding the fiber supply is in constant motion. It is either drawing fibers out or feeding yarn onto the bobbin.

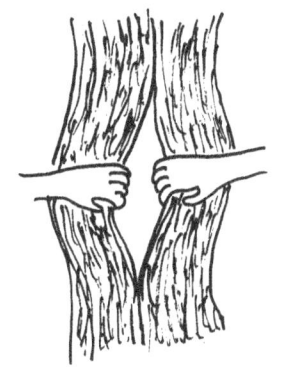

DIVIDING THE CARDED BATT PRIOR TO SPINNING.

After spinning, skein and tie the yarn for finishing. The importance of yarn finishing cannot be stressed too much for singles knitting yarns. The bane of knitting with a singles yarn is a bias twist in the garment. To avoid this, set the twist after spinning, and for further insurance, tension the yarn firmly while knitting! Setting is achieved by means of moisture, heat, tension, or some combination thereof. A combination of heat and moisture often gives the best results, although some spinners have found that moisture alone is sufficient.

A simmer bath is highly recommended for setting twist. To minimize crowding, place the skeined and tied yarn in a large pot such as a large enamel canner. Fill the pot with warm water and sufficient liquid detergent for a typical washing. Place the pot on a burner and heat slowly to a simmer (about 180°). Do not stir the yarn, but turn it gently every few minutes so that the heat is evenly distributed. Once the simmer point is reached, preferably over a twenty minute period, turn the heat off and allow the bath to cool while the yarn soaks. When the water is comfortably warm to the hand, drain the pot and rinse the skeins. Excess water can be extracted in the spin cycle of the washer, if desired.

Stretch the skeins between your hands to remove kinks in the yarn by placing both hands within the circumference of the skein and snapping outward vigorously. Repeat the action several times, working around the skein.

Setting the Twist

DIRECTION OF TWIST: RESULTS FROM THE DIRECTION THAT THE DRIVE WHEEL TURNS WHILE SPINNING THE YARN. IF THE DRIVE WHEEL TURNS COUNTER-CLOCKWISE, THE YARN IS SPUN WITH AN S-TWIST. IF IT TURNS CLOCKWISE, A Z-TWIST RESULTS. THE Z-TWIST IS COMMONLY USED FOR SINGLES KNITTING YARNS, BOTH HANDSPUN AND COMMERCIALLY PRODUCED. THIS IS ALSO TRUE FOR MOST SALISH YARNS.

STRAIGHTENING THE SKEIN AFTER FINISHING.

Drying the yarn under tension at this point will reduce loft and is not necessary. After finishing and drying, the yarn is ready to be rolled into gigantic balls in preparation for knitting.

For the Non-Spinner

A well-made handspun yarn adds another dimension to the handknit sweater, a subtle quality for which there is no substitute. There is no commercially-spun equivalent to this type of handspun yarn. If such a yarn were readily available, Salish knitters would surely be using this shortcut in producing their sweaters. The non-spinner does have options, however. Some of the Salish craftspeople sell their yarns as well as their sweaters. Or, one can seek out a handspinner with an Indian-head spinner and the necessary skills to spin these yarns.

There are some commercially-prepared bulky yarns available which can be used in Salish patterns. A bulky spun singles yarn from White Buffalo is the best alternative. In addition, there are several suppliers of 4-6 ply unspun roving-type yarns (including White Buffalo). These yarns have little twist but will give fair results if very firmly knit. Be aware that their durability is limited and that pilling can be a problem. Also, they do not hold their shape in long-term use as do the handspuns.

CHAPTER SIX
Knitting Techniques

To the casual eye, the Salish sweaters appear much alike, yet by studying the garments closely, one sees rich diversity in technique and design! These sweaters are created by the hands of many individual knitters who put their own personal imprint on their work. Strong familial traits emerged as the techniques were passed from generation to generation, setting each family's work apart in subtle ways from the knitters who lived down the road. Often, the movements of family members around the entire region can be traced by way of nuances in their knitting style, establishing the family ties from the mother at Cowichan Station to her daughters in nearby Ladysmith and over to Laidlaw on the mainland of British Columbia and then down to Anacortes and Seattle in Washington.

The sweaters do share common elements, however. They are seamless garments, knit on double-pointed needles, with a V-neck and shawl collar. They are knit of handspun singles yarn in two or three natural wool colors worked in bands of geometric design, with representational designs replacing a portion of the geometrics in many cases. Originally, the sweaters were pullovers, but today most are cardigans due to consumer preference.

Multiple double-pointed needles (five or more) are the tools folk knitters of all cultures have used to construct seamless garments. This is true of Salish knitters, also. Their early needles were laboriously hand carved from bone or local wood, yew being preferred. The Salish were familiar with the qualities of yew from its earlier use in bows where strength and flexibility were important. These qualities are also attributes of a good knitting needle.

Today's knitters use commercially-produced needles. They still prefer to use double-pointed needles in preference to modern circular ones. Some feel that the heavy yarn is more easily accommodated by multiple needles. Others indicate that multiple needles allow them to divide a pattern into sections established by the regular repeat of the geometric designs, thus enabling the knitter to maintain the continuity more easily. Typically,

NORA GEORGE EXPLAINING THE SLANTED POCKET TREATMENT THAT SHE IS USING ON A CURRENT PROJECT, A METHOD THAT SHE CREDITS TO HER OLDER SISTER. NOTE THE CENTER FRONT EDGING WORKED IN TWO COLORS.

KEYS TO SYMBOLS IN ILLUSTRATIONS

- DENOTES CHANGE IN NUMBER OF STITCHES, INCREASE OR DECREASE AS APPROPRIATE.

ℓ DENOTES CAST-ON OR PICKED-UP STITCHES.

the sweaters are knit on needles (usually an American size 8 to 10 or metric size 5 to 6 mm) to produce a firm gauge, 4 to 5 stitches to the inch in the older heavyweight yarns and 2.5 to 3.5 stitches to the inch in today's bulkier yarns.

The sweater is knit in the classic circular technique of the peasant populations of Europe, with one exception. Many European color-stranded garments were worked in the round throughout with provisions made for cutting the armholes and, in the case of a cardigan, the front opening. The common Scottish term for this provision is "steek," a term also in use in the United States. This technique is not practiced among the Indian knitters, but rather the knitting is worked back and forth where openings are required. Steeking was not practiced on the British gansey, the probable source of the basic structural techniques for the Indian sweater, for it served no viable purpose for the textured designs on that type of fisherman's sweater. When color stranding, steeking allows the face of the design to be visible at all times to the knitter, greatly increasing knitting speed. Therefore, steeking was often practiced on the

 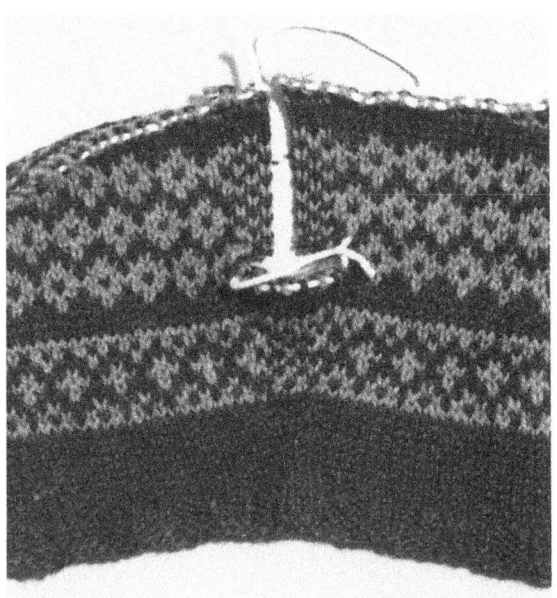

STEEK USED IN TRADITIONAL FAIR ISLE SWEATER, BOTH BEFORE CUTTING (LEFT) AND AFTER (RIGHT). USING THE STEEK TO FILL IN THE OPENING ALLOWS THE KNITTING TO CONTINUE IN THE ROUND. THE LOWER HALF OF A GUSSET IS WORKED BELOW THE STEEK. NOTE THE BREAK FROM GEOMETRIC PATTERN TO CHECKERBOARD STITCHES USED IN THE GUSSET. GUSSET STITCHES ARE PLACED ON A HOLDER WHEN THE UNDERARM DEPTH IS REACHED. NEW STITCHES ARE CAST ON TO CLOSE THIS OPENING. THE STEEK STITCHES ARE ALSO WORKED IN CHECKERBOARD. AFTER THE BODY IS COMPLETED, THE STEEK IS CUT, THE SLEEVE KNITTED, AND FINALLY, THE STEEK TURNED BACK AND WORKED DOWN INTO THE BODY.

Fair Isle jerseys. The technique was valuable for the fine European yarns, but not suitable for the thick yarns used by the Salish knitters, for it would add tremendous bulk where cut and turned under. There are Indian sweaters on the market which have been cut, but no provision has been made for the cutting, so a raw edge is exposed at the zipper. These are sweaters that have been converted to cardigans by dealers.

The earliest Salish sweaters were pullovers, but when knitters began to take commissions for these garments, many consumers preferred a cardigan style. This remains true today. To make a pullover, the knitter casts on and joins in the round, knitting in the classic circular style. To appropriately construct a cardigan, the knitter casts on in the same manner and then knits back and forth from the center front rather than joining the circle – still creating a seamless garment, but one that does not require cutting.

Older cardigans were made with a button overlap, whereas today the standard closure is a heavy-duty zipper stitched into the center front opening. When an overlap was needed for buttons, a six-stitch section of garter stitch was established at both edges, with the buttonholes worked at appropriate locations as the knitting progressed. Since an overlap is not needed for a zipper, many knitters today work back and forth, slipping the first stitch of every row. This creates a firm selvage and controls rolling at the edge. Those who do not slip the first stitch will often finish the work with a crochet edge to achieve the same end, although this is not as effective. Others prefer to work the traditional garter stitch edge over the first two to four stitches at both sides. In this case, the first stitch may or may not be slipped to firm up the edge. No sweaters were found with a crochet edge applied to the garter stitch border.

Two-Stitch Border

A unique edge treatment, seen only in the work of the finest knitters, principally in one family, develops a decorative two-stitch front-edge border in two colors. This treatment helps to

Cardigan Edges

TWO-COLOR EDGE TREATMENT WORKED AT THE CENTER FRONT OPENING AND AROUND THE COLLAR. NOTE THAT THE FIRST STITCH OF EACH ROW IS SLIPPED.

KNITTING TECHNIQUES

camouflage soiling that might otherwise show in a light-colored sweater.

This pattern consists of working two rows in the main color followed by two rows in the contrast color over the first two stitches at each edge. It appears more complex because the first stitch of every row is slipped. Once established in this pattern, the knitter maintains it until the base of the collar is reached. These two stitches will then be set aside for the collar edging.

INSTRUCTIONS: *Two-Stitch Border*

- Cast on the required number of stitches for the lower band of the sweater.
- Leave a long tail (about 2 yards) at the end of the cast on, sufficient to work the border for the total length of the zipper opening. Additional length can be added by splicing, if necessary.
- Work ribbing, being sure to begin and end with knit stitches at each edge.
- Work the cast-on and the first row in the contrast color: slip the first stitch, work up to, but not including the final stitch. Use main color on the last stitch of the first row.
- Break contrast color off here, leaving a strand long enough to work the two-stitch edging up the entire zipper opening.
- Turn the work and slip the first stitch (main color).
- Taking care always to twist the yarn being picked up from under the dropped strand on color changes, work the second stitch in contrast color, then change back to main color to work across to the final two stitches.
- Work the next-to-last stitch in contrast color, using the long tail from the cast-on, and the final stitch in the main color.
- Turn, slip the first stitch and work row in main color, up to the final stitch, which is worked in contrast color.
- Turn, slip the first stitch (contrast color) work row in the main color up to the final stitch, which is worked in the contrast color.
- Turn, slip first stitch (contrast color), work second stitch in contrast color, returning to main color for all but the final two stitches.
- Work next-to-last stitch in contrast color and the last stitch in the main color.
- Turn, slip first stitch (main color), work the second stitch in the contrast color. Return to main color until the final two stitches (worked in contrast color and main color, respectively.)

This treatment is very effective, but as it is time consuming, many Indian knitters prefer to use one of the methods described earlier. The same edging is equally effective on collars worked in ribbing. In that case, the last row and the bind-off row of the collar back must be worked in a corresponding pattern with the knit stitches in the one color and the purl stitches in the other.

Sweater Body

A deep welt of ribbing serves as a lower band at the base of the sweater. In sweaters made in the 1920s and 30s when finer yarns were utilized, a knit-one, purl-one ribbing was standard on most sweaters. Today a knit-two, purl-two ribbing is most common, although some knitters prefer to use a knit-two, purl-one ribbing.

In the older sweaters, the addition of a few stitches above the ribbing for additional ease was not a common practice. Most knitters now add four to six ease stitches. This is sufficient to control flare in the ribbing that often develops as the ribbing stretches out with continual use of the garment. The body is then worked in stockinette stitch to the base of the armholes.

Pockets

Many of the sweaters do not have pockets. For those that do, pockets are placed with the top edge just above the second geometric band. (See page 77 for details of design placement.) The earliest pockets were often squares with a garter stitch top that was applied to the surface of the sweater. As the pocket position was within a band of design, the knitter had to work the pattern on the patch pocket to match that of the design band. Horizontal pockets are the most common style, and easiest to fit into the designs. Slanted pockets are less common, requiring more space between the design bands.

CARDIGAN WITH HORIZONTAL POCKETS IN THREE COLORS, 1986. COURTESY OF EVA WILLIAMS, DUNCAN, BRITISH COLUMBIA.

Horizontal Slash Pockets

Today, horizontal openings are worked into the sweater body, finished with either a small ribbing or garter stitch welt to match the collar that is planned. Pocket liners are knit for the opening established by binding off the welt. The stitches of the pocket liner replace those removed by casting off the welt and the body of the sweater is continued to the underarm.

A.   B.

PICKING UP STITCHES THROUGH PURL HEADS

A. PURL HEAD ENTERED FROM TOP TO BOTTOM, NEEDLE WRAPPED AS TO PURL.
B. WRAP DRAWN THROUGH TO FORM PURL LOOP.

INSTRUCTIONS: *Horizontal Slash Pockets*

- Locate the position of the pockets (see illustration) and work a welt over the next four rows.
- Bind off the welt stitches in the sweater body for pocket opening.
- Cast on stitches for a separate liner, or pick up stitches purlwise on wrong side, just above the ribbing and directly below the bound-off stitches, by inserting the needle through the purl heads. Leave a long tail of yarn (about 12 inches).
- Knit a panel in stockinette stitch to the depth necessary to reach the top of the pocket welt.
- Break off yarn, leaving a 12-inch tail of yarn.
- Insert the pocket stitches into the sweater body to replace those bound off for the welt.
- Continue knitting the sweater body.

FINISHING: Use the two long tails of yarn to secure pocket lining to sweater body.

HORIZONTAL SLASH POCKETS

A. WORK DIVIDED INTO 5 PARTS FOR A CARDIGAN, 4 FOR A PULLOVER (#S 1 AND 5 BECOME ONE UNIT). A WELT OF GARTER STITCH OR RIBBING WORKED ON OUTSIDE.

B. POCKET LINER KNIT WITH NUMBER OF STITCHES BOUND OFF FOR WELT. POSITION OF LINER AND FINAL POCKET APPEARANCE

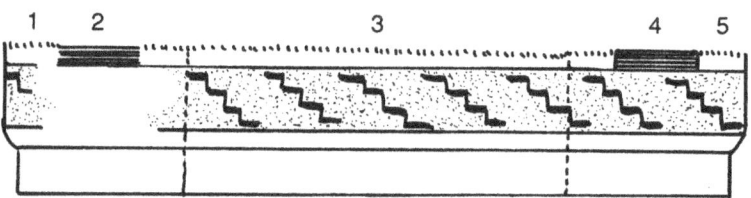

A

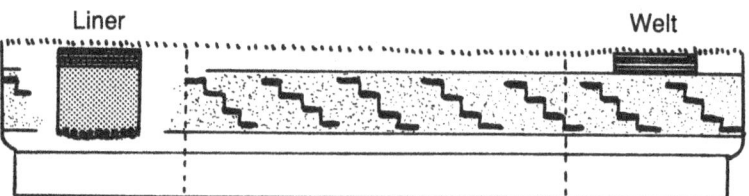

B

Reinforcement

Some knitters work one extra stitch at each side of the pocket liner. These stitches are overlapped at each end when joining the flap into the main body to reinforce an area of potential stress.

Slanted Pockets

A few of the more accomplished knitters have begun to experiment with slanting the pocket openings. They feel that a slant is more desirable both in terms of comfort and durability. Warming hands in horizontal pockets places more stress on the knit stitiches at each pocket edge. Slanting the pocket reduces the stress. The horizontal pocket is easier to place between geometric design bands, but with careful planning the slanted pocket can be used on most sweaters. Slanted shaping may be worked on front pocket edges only for a pocket with a vertical liner, or on both front and back edges for a pocket with a slanted liner.

BACK AND FRONT VIEWS OF AN EARLY CARDIGAN WITH DESIGN WORKED IN BROWN ON WHITE, REMAINDER OF SWEATER IN HEATHERED YARN. GARTER STITCH WAS USED FOR LOWER BAND AND POCKET WELT, BUTTON OVERLAP AND COLLAR. NECK IS SHAPED WITH THREE DECREASES ON EACH SIDE OF NECK EDGE. ARMHOLES WERE WORKED STRAIGHT AND SLEEVES WERE PICKED UP AND WORKED DOWN. THIS SWEATER WAS PURCHASED IN THE COWICHAN AREA OF VANCOUVER ISLAND IN AUGUST, 1938. COURTESY OF THE U.B.C. MUSEUM OF ANTHROPOLOGY, VANCOUVER, BRITISH COLUMBIA.

KNITTING TECHNIQUES

INSTRUCTIONS: *Slanted Pockets with Vertical Liners*

- Divide the work into three sections for a cardigan, two for a pullover. (see diagram below.)
- Work shaded area A1 to desired depth, decreasing pocket edge every knit row with a Sl1, K1, PSSO (left-slanting) decrease.
- Repeat on section A3, using a K2 tog. (right-slanting) decrease.
- Work the linings as for the horizontal pocket, casting on or picking up the purl heads at the base of the pocket just above the ribbing.
- Knit pocket linings in stockinette stitch.
- Incorporate the linings into the sweater body when it reaches the base of the slant.
- Knit back and forth on these stitches to a depth equal to the center front depth.
- Join front section(s) and continue to knit total body stitches.

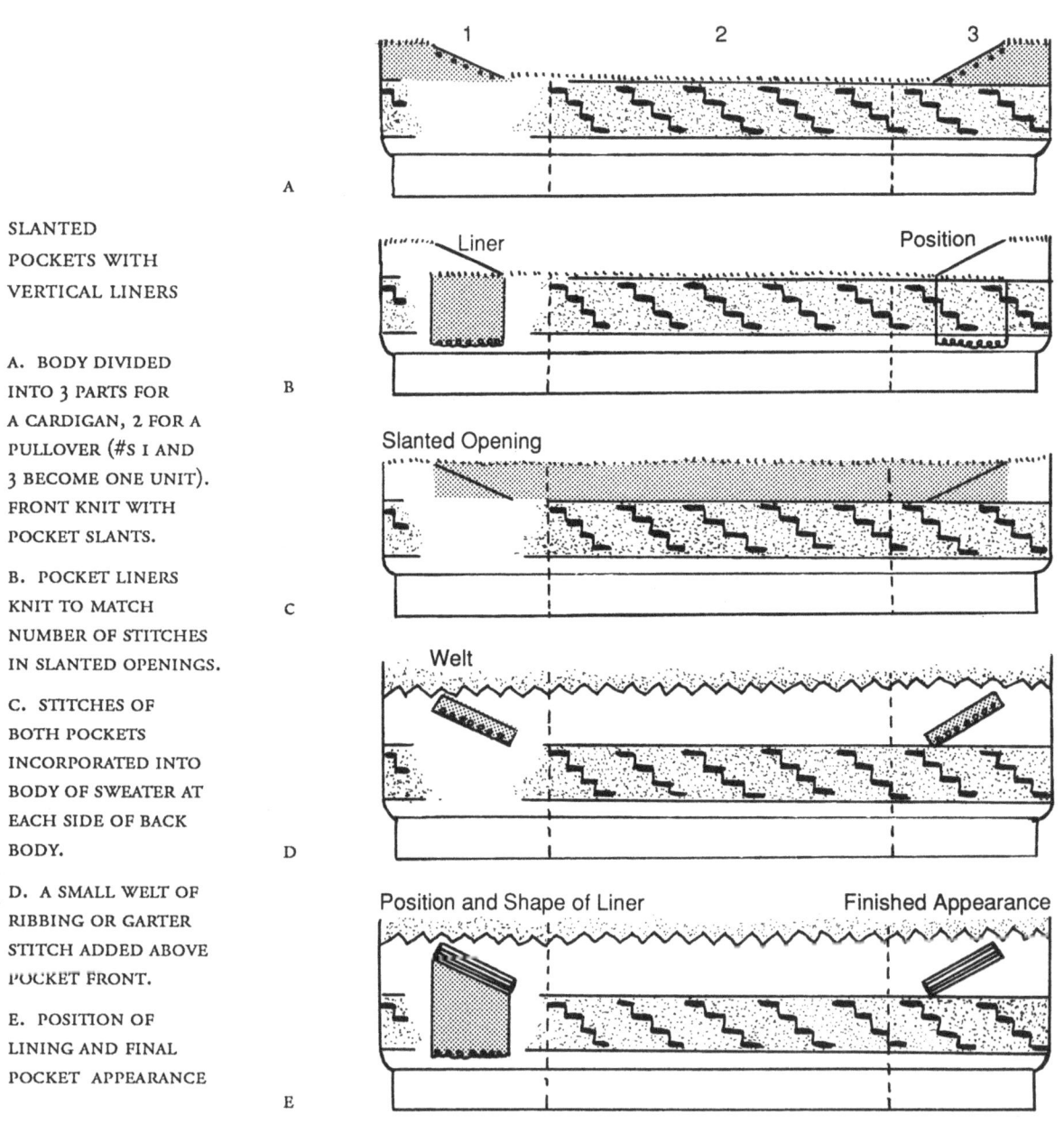

SLANTED POCKETS WITH VERTICAL LINERS

A. BODY DIVIDED INTO 3 PARTS FOR A CARDIGAN, 2 FOR A PULLOVER (#S 1 AND 3 BECOME ONE UNIT). FRONT KNIT WITH POCKET SLANTS.

B. POCKET LINERS KNIT TO MATCH NUMBER OF STITCHES IN SLANTED OPENINGS.

C. STITCHES OF BOTH POCKETS INCORPORATED INTO BODY OF SWEATER AT EACH SIDE OF BACK BODY.

D. A SMALL WELT OF RIBBING OR GARTER STITCH ADDED ABOVE POCKET FRONT.

E. POSITION OF LINING AND FINAL POCKET APPEARANCE

INSTRUCTIONS: *Slanted Pockets with Slanted Liners*

- Divide body into sections as for slanted pockets with vertical liners. (see diagram).
- Work shaded area A1 to desired depth decreasing pocket edge every knit row with a left-slanting decrease. Repeat on A3 using right-slanted decrease.
- Work sweater back (shaded in diagram) back and forth, making a corresponding slant on the edge of the pockets by *increasing* at each end of every knit row with a backward loop.
- When both units match, rejoin the work and continue the body.
- As both front and back pocket edges are slanted, pick up stitches along the *back* edge and work down to make the pocket lining. In this case, not only the pocket opening slants, but the lining will also slant at the same angle that the hand fits into a pocket.
- Work lining to desired depth; bind off at base.
- Add a welt edging if desired by picking up stitches at lower edge of opening and working up to desired depth.

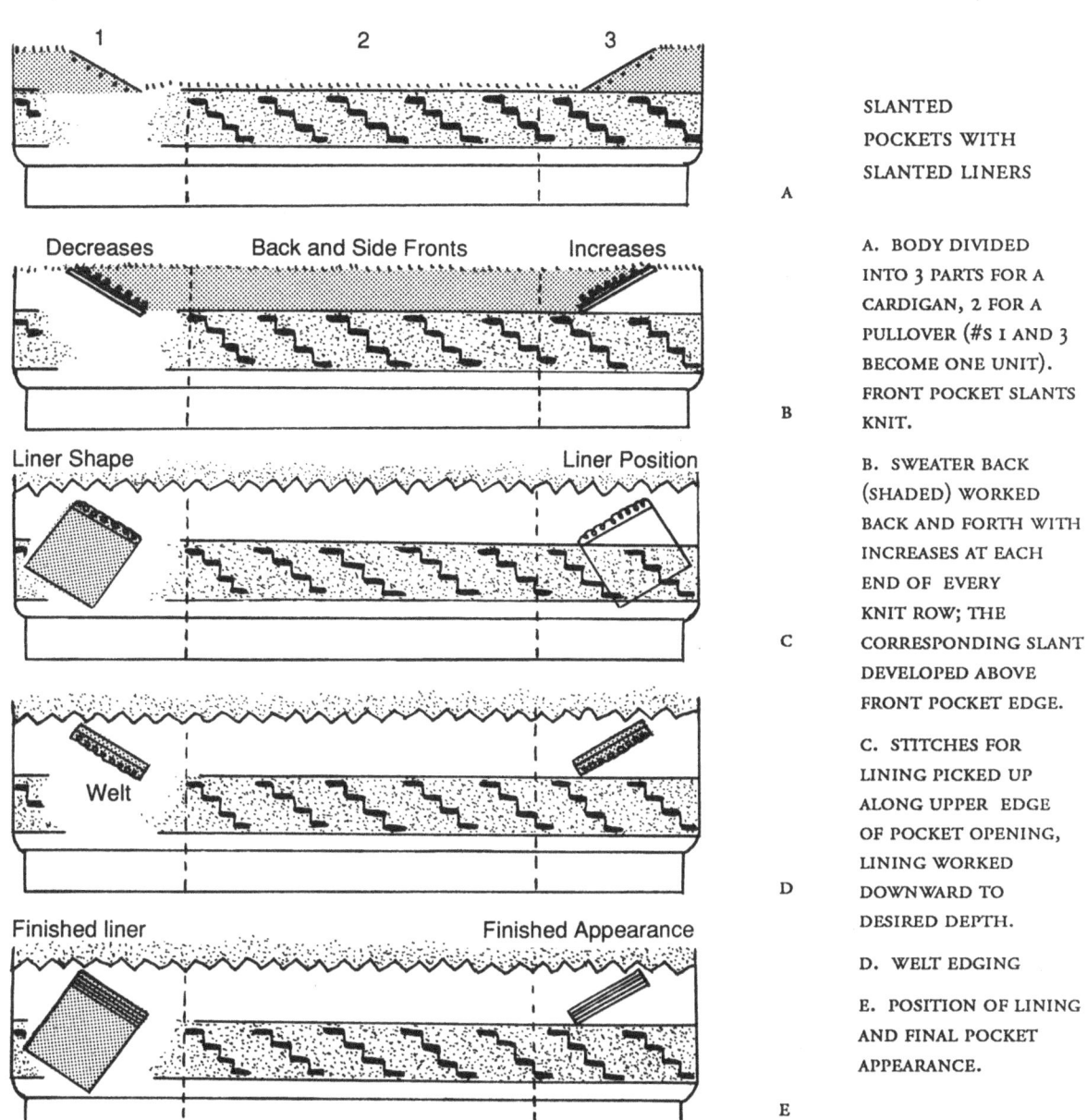

SLANTED POCKETS WITH SLANTED LINERS

A. BODY DIVIDED INTO 3 PARTS FOR A CARDIGAN, 2 FOR A PULLOVER (#S 1 AND 3 BECOME ONE UNIT). FRONT POCKET SLANTS KNIT.

B. SWEATER BACK (SHADED) WORKED BACK AND FORTH WITH INCREASES AT EACH END OF EVERY KNIT ROW; THE CORRESPONDING SLANT DEVELOPED ABOVE FRONT POCKET EDGE.

C. STITCHES FOR LINING PICKED UP ALONG UPPER EDGE OF POCKET OPENING, LINING WORKED DOWNWARD TO DESIRED DEPTH.

D. WELT EDGING

E. POSITION OF LINING AND FINAL POCKET APPEARANCE.

KNITTING TECHNIQUES

Pocket Borders

After the body has been completed, pocket borders may be added, if desired, by working a small welt across the top edge of the pocket. An edge treatment is not necessary, as the decreasing that forms the pocket also stabilizes the edge.

Completing the Body

The body is knit in stockinette stitch to the armhole on the number of stitches established above the ribbing. On some of the older sweaters, especially when no stitches were added above the ribbing, a few knitters would add one stitch at the center point of the underarm two or three times. This might be considered a modified version of the gusset traditionally found on British gansey sweaters.

Armholes and Neck

To form an armhole opening, the work is divided at the underarm, and the front and back worked separately from this point upward. Usually, eight or ten stitches are removed to a stitch holder at the underarm, half coming

---

ARMHOLE OPTIONS

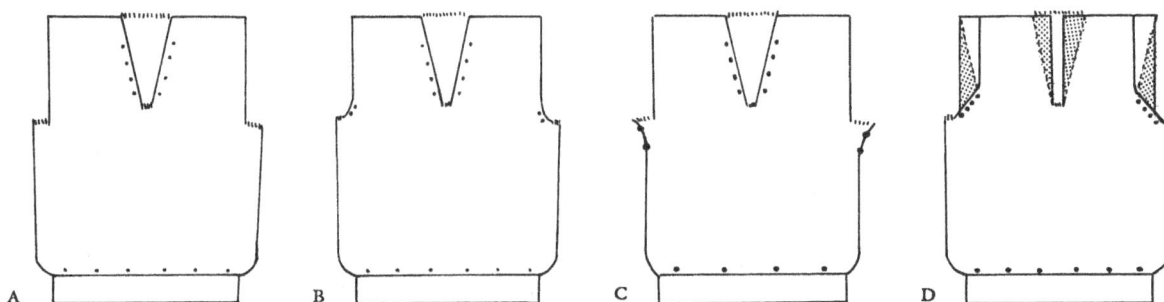

A. SQUARE ARMHOLES: (MOST COMMON STYLE). UNDERARM STITCHES PLACED ON HOLDERS, HALF FROM FRONT, HALF FROM BACK. ARMHOLE EDGES ARE STRAIGHT.

B. SHAPED ARMHOLES: FEWER STITCHES PLACED ON HOLDERS. DECREASES MADE ON EVERY OTHER ROW ON THE BACK AND FRONT ARMHOLE EDGES. THIS ARMHOLE MAY BE USED WITH A SHAPED SLEEVE CAP.

C. SEMI-GUSSET ARMHOLES: USED WHEN FEWER STITCHES ARE ADDED FOR EASE ABOVE RIBBING. ONE STITCH AT ARMHOLE CENTER INCREASED 2 OR 3 TIMES. (GOOD FIT FOR SLENDER BROAD-SHOULDERED FIGURE).

D. SHAPED ARMHOLES CREATING V-NECK: (DEPENDS ON ELASTICITY OF THE KNIT FABRIC TO WORK.) NECK EDGE IS NOT SHAPED, MERELY DIVIDED. FRONT ARMHOLE EDGE IS RAPIDLY DECREASED. AT SHOULDER JOIN, THE FRONT ARMHOLE EDGE IS DRAWN OUTWARD TO CREATE V-NECK. FEWER STITCHES ARE SET ASIDE FROM FRONT UNDER-ARM, MORE FROM THE BACK. DECREASES ARE MADE ON EVERY ROW AT ARMHOLE EDGE UNTIL TOTAL DECREASES PLUS CENTER FRONT STITCHES EQUALS THE NUMBER OF BACK NECK STITCHES. THIS UNUSUAL SHAPING IS SEEN MOST FREQUENTLY ON CHILDREN'S SWEATERS.

from the side front and half coming from the side back. Typically, the armholes of the Indian sweaters are not shaped, but rather worked straight for their total depth. A few knitters opt for shaping the armhole with several decreases on every other row, thereby following the body contours more closely. This treatment is most effective if a small cap is built on the upper sleeve (described below). Usually three stitches are decreased at both the front and back of the armhole for this type of treatment, with fewer stitches removed at the underarm.

Older sweaters often had no shaping for the armhole or neck. The garter stitch overlaps on a cardigan, usually six stitches on each side, were removed to a holder to form the base of the collar. The knitting was continued to the total shoulder depth. As no shaping had occurred on the front neck opening, the back neck was relatively narrow, equaling the total number of stitches removed from the front for the collar base.

The pullover had six to eight stitches removed at the center front to form the base of the collar. To accommodate the need for more back neck stitches, underarm stitches were not taken equally from the front and back halves. Instead, more were taken out of the front side — as many as necessary to allow for at least ten back neck stitches.

V-Neck

Knitters today prefer to do some minimal shaping of the V-neck on both the cardigan and the pullover. Whereas on the older sweaters, the depth of the collar equaled the armhole

---

V-NECK OPTIONS

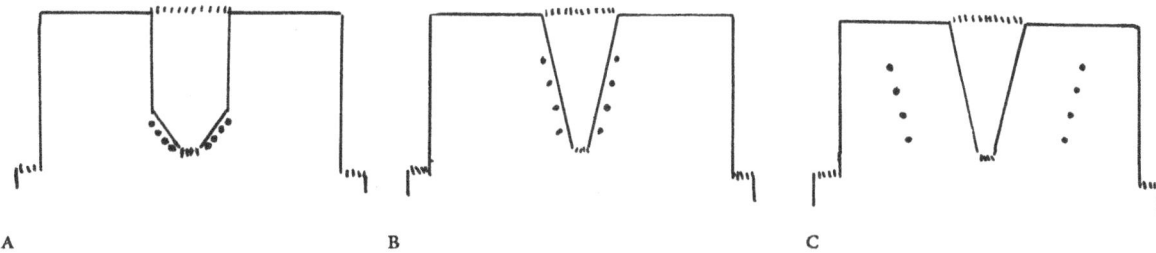

A

B

C

A. DECREASES AT BASE OF POINT.
B. DECREASES EVENLY SPACED UP NECK EDGE.
C. DECREASES BETWEEN NECK EDGE AND ARMHOLE EDGE.

depth, many now prefer to work an additional inch or two before beginning the base of the collar. Some even bring the base of the collar to the base of the neck itself. When dividing the work for a pullover, most knitters set aside two stitches from each side of the center front to be used as the base of the collar. In the case of the cardigan, if a specific edge treatment has been used, these edge stitches are removed to a holder for the collar base. Otherwise, the collar base of the cardigan is handled like the pullover, with two to four stitches removed at each side. In a few cases, the front edge of the cardigan has been worked even, with no stitches set aside to form the base of the collar.

Many knitters, especially those who slip the first stitch of the cardigan edge, will also slip the first stitch of the V-neck in order to simplify the pick-up of the collar stitches. Others prefer to work all stitches at the neck edge, claiming that the neck edge needs more elasticity, not a firm slip-stitch edge. The V-neck is shaped by decreasing the number of stitches on each side several times.

Neck Decreases

The decreases may be closely spaced and only at the point of the V, or they may be evenly spaced at wider intervals up the entire depth of the neck. If widely spaced, the decreases may be placed at the neck edge or they may be centered on each side front (although not in the horizontal design band). Regardless of the positioning of the decreases the number is limited, depending upon how many stitches were removed from the front. If two stitches are removed at each side front, there are usually four decreases on each side front, again leaving twelve stitches for the back neck, while very large sweaters might have fourteen to sixteen, in each case necessitating an adjustment of the number of decreases at the neck. The opposite holds true for a child's sweater.

Alternative Method

An interesting but less common system of V-neck shaping involves shaping only the armhole. The center front is worked straight and drawn aside to form a V-shaped opening when the shoulders are joined. The underarm stitches are removed and decreases are worked at the base of the front armhole edge until enough stitches are removed to allow for twelve back neck stitches on an average sweater. This method is used most often in small sweaters. See child's sweater pictured on the front cover.

Although early publications on Cowichan sweaters have indicated that the shoulders were shaped by dividing them into three sections and binding them off in stair-step fashion, ending with a sewn shoulder seam, none of the sweaters studied fit this description. Furthermore, none of the knitters interviewed had any knowledge of such a technique having existed among the early knitters. Shaping shoulders in stair-step manner is a typical method used in modern printed patterns, but was apparently not used in the early folk sweaters. Three shoulder joins are described below. They produce three different decorative braid effects.

Bind-Off Together

In both old and new sweaters, front and back shoulder stitches are often bound off together in the manner of the old British gansey.

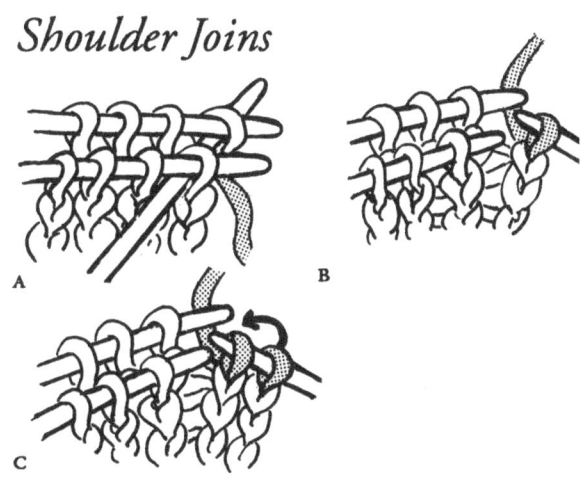

Shoulder Joins

BIND-OFF TOGETHER SHOULDER JOIN

A. A THIRD NEEDLE ENTERS THE FIRST STITCH OF BOTH PIECES.

B. FIRST STITCH FORMED ON WORKING NEEDLE.

C. A SECOND STITCH FORMED ON WORKING NEEDLE AND PASSED OVER TO BIND OFF.

INSTRUCTIONS: *Bind-Off Together, Three-Needle Method*

- Place the front and back shoulders together, each with the stitches mounted on their respective needles. With a third needle, enter the first stitch on the front needle knitwise, and also enter the first stitch on the back needle knitwise.

- Draw a loop through both stitches to mount one new stitch on the working needle.

- Repeat with the second stitch on both the front and back, mounting a second new stitch on the working needle.

- Bind the first stitch off by passing it over the second stitch on the working needle.

- Repeat as established, until all the stitches have been removed.

On many of the sweaters studied, the shoulders are bound off together beginning at the left side, with the bind-off continuing across the back neck stitches and then across the right side. The back neck stitches may be picked up from the bound-off edge for the collar base. On other sweaters, the first shoulder is bound off as described, the back neck stitches are worked across but not bound

KNITTING TECHNIQUES

off, then the second shoulder is bound off. The back neck stitches are in place for the base of the collar in this case.

Those who bind off the entire area, including the back neck stitches claim this method makes a more comfortable garment, as the entire back is stabilized with the bound-off edge. Those who prefer to set aside the back neck stitches for the base of the collar feel this makes the sweater fit better as it is more elastic, allowing the subsequent collar to follow the curvature of the neck.

Regardless of which method is used, this treatment can be worked on the surface to create a decorative ridge, or on the inside to develop a nearly invisible shoulder join.

SHOULDER OPTIONS

A   B   C

A SHOULDER WITH FRONT AND BACK STITCHES BOUND OFF TOGETHER ON THE SURFACE OF THE SWEATER. THIS TREATMENT MAY ALSO BE WORKED FROM THE INSIDE OF THE GARMENT, MAKING A NEARLY INVISIBLE JOIN ON THE SURFACE.

B. SHOULDER WITH DOUBLE BIND-OFF. FRONT AND BACK SHOULDER STITCHES ARE BOUND OFF SIMULTANEOUSLY USING THE SAME YARN. TWO SEPARATE, BUT JOINED, RIDGES ARE FORMED.

C. SHOULDER WITH TRIPLE BIND-OFF. FRONT AND BACK STITCHES ARE BOUND OFF SEPARATELY. NEW STITCHES ARE PICKED UP BEHIND THE BIND-OFF CHAIN AND BOUND OFF TOGETHER.

Double Bind-Off

By 1950, another shoulder treatment began to appear on Indian sweaters. This treatment appears unique to the Salish, one of their many contributions to knitting techniques. In this case, each shoulder is bound off at the same time, using the same strand of yarn, but they are *not* bound off together. Rather than a single bound off edge, two bound off edges lie side by side, connected by the bind-off yarn. Some knitters work this technique on two pairs of needles in the old way. Most prefer to simplify the work by using only three needles. Both methods are described below.

This shoulder treatment is always worked on the surface to take advantage of the decorative ridge it forms. As with the older binding-off-together finish, the back neck stitches can either be bound off for a firm edge, or worked across in purl to the second shoulder, depending on the knitter's preference.

Four-Needle Method

This is the traditonal method.

INSTRUCTIONS: *Double Bind-Off, Four Needles*
- Place front shoulder stitches on one needle and the back shoulder stitches on another needle.
- Working with two sets of needles and one strand of yarn, knit the first stitch on the front needles, and purl the first stitch on the back needles.
- Knit second front needle stitch, pass first stitch over it – one front stitch bound off.
- Purl the second back needle stitch and pass the first back stitch over it – one back stitch bound off.
- Continue in this manner, knitting and binding off one stitch on the front, then purling and binding off one stitch on the back, all with the same strand of yarn.

Three-Needle Method

Many knitters have simplified the double bind-off by using only one working needle, and rotating it to bind off both the front and back. This allows the knitter to tension the yarn more evenly, without the frustration of dropping needles. The strand of yarn remains *between* the two needles, and the third working needle (a short, straight cable needle of appropriate size, if available), is rotated first clockwise to the front, then counterclockwise to the back. The needle slides back and forth to bring the tip within working distance of the stitches on both the front and back needles.

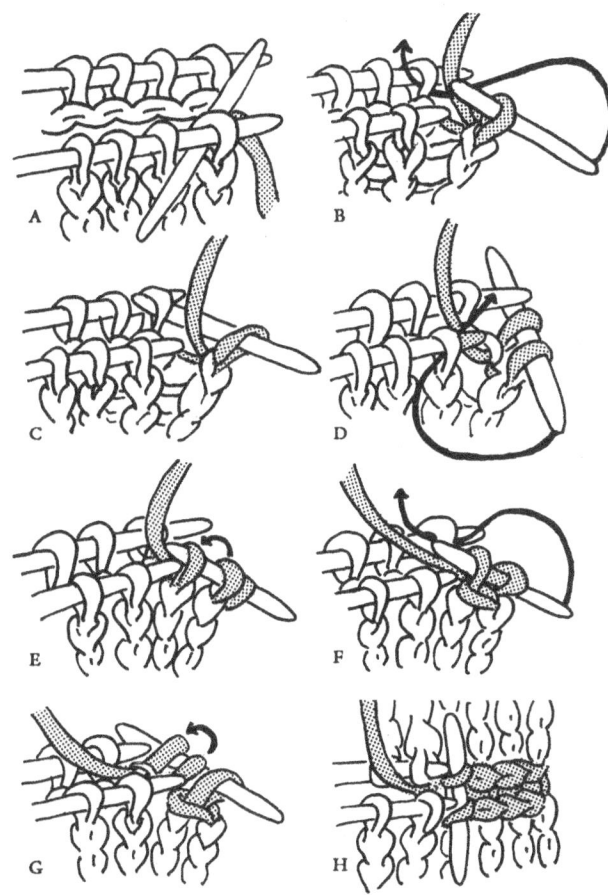

DOUBLE BIND-OFF SHOULDER JOIN, THREE-NEEDLES

A. ONE STITCH KNIT ON FRONT NEEDLE.

B. WORKING NEEDLE TURNED COUNTERCLOCKWISE TO BACK STITCHES.

C. ONE STICH PURLED FROM BACK NEEDLE.

D. WORKING NEEDLE TURNED CLOCKWISE TO FRONT NEEDLE, ONE STITCH KNIT ON FRONT.

E. FIRST KNIT STITCH PASSED OVER THE SECOND KNIT STITCH TO BIND OFF ONE ON FRONT.

F. WORKING NEEDLE TURNED COUNTERCLOCKWISE TO BACK, ONE STITCH PURLED.

G. FIRST PURL STITCH OVER SECOND TO BIND OFF ONE ON BACK.

H. BIND-OFF ALTERNATED, KNIT ON FRONT, PURL ON BACK.

KNITTING TECHNIQUES

INSTRUCTIONS: *Double Bind-Off, Three-Needles*

- Knit the first stitch from the front needle, then rotate the other tip of the working needle counterclockwise into purl position for the back and purl one from the back.
- Rotate the working needle clockwise to bring the front tip into position to knit one from the front needle, passing the first front stitch over to bind off.
- Rotate the working needle counterclockwise to bring the back tip of the working needle into purl position, purl one stitch and pass the first back stitch over for the bind-off.
- Continue the process until only one front stitch and one back stitch remain to be bound off.
- Knit these last two stitches together, break off the yarn and draw the end through the resulting loop.

Triple Bind-Off

A third shoulder finish, seen in the sweaters produced by members of one extended family, produces a wide decorative ridge with a triple bind-off. To achieve this finish, the knitter must first bind off the front shoulders and the entire back separately.

This shoulder treatment is always worked on the surface of the shoulder for a decorative finish that is extremely stable.

INSTRUCTIONS: *Triple Bind-Off*

- Bind off each piece separately.
- To join the pieces, front to back, pick up the purl heads of the bind-off row. To correctly mount the picked up stitches, work from the right edge to the left edge with the chain of the bind-off facing you (right side facing).
- Pick up the front shoulder stitches on one needle, the back stitches on another. The front and back shoulders, with the stitches picked up on two needles, are then bound off again together, wrong sides together.
- With a third needle, enter the first front stitch and then the first back stitch knitwise, drawing a loop through both stitches.
- Repeat to have two stitches on the working needle. Pass the first stitch over the second to complete the bind-off of that stitch.
- Repeat the process until all of the stitches have been bound off together.

Note: The directional lay of the bind-off lies in the opposite direction on the back. To avoid this, bind off the back in purl.

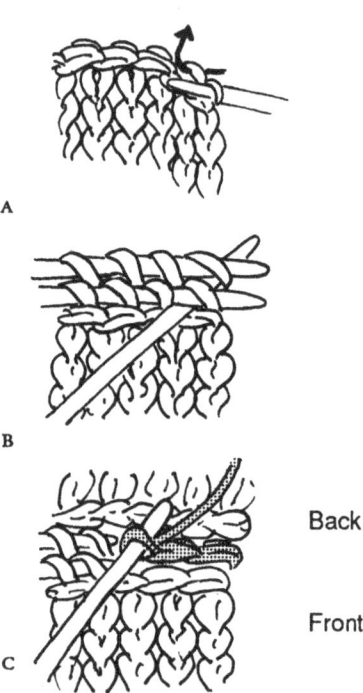

TRIPLE BIND-OFF

A. PURL HEAD PICKED UP BEHIND BIND-OFF CHAIN.
B. FIRST STITCHES ON FRONT AND BACK NEEDLES KNIT TOGETHER.
C. BIND-OFF SEQUENCE COMPLETED.

Shawl Collars

The wide shawl collar can be worked in garter stitch or in a knit one, purl one ribbing. Some references indicate that collars have also been done in basket stitch, but none were found worked in this manner. The collar may be worked in one of two basic ways: (1) a seamless collar worked in three units that are joined together during the knitting, and (2) a continuous one-piece collar.

Three-Unit Collar

The earliest shawl collars were worked in three units, but were seamless. Early studies indicated that the collar back was worked first, then the two side fronts picked up along the collar edges and worked down to the point. No examples were found of this construction, and none of the knitters interviewed were aware of any collars having been worked in this order. A shawl collar can be developeed in this order, but it requires that an increase be made at the end of each row on the back collar stitches. On the collar front, it would require that the knitter first pick up a stitch at the neck edge and join it with the last collar stitch on one row, and then decrease one stitch at the beginning of the next row. Either an increase or a decrease is worked on *every row* of the collar. Every such increase and decrease are extra labor, consuming precious time, and therefore this method is not practical for someone trying to earn an income by knitting.

Collar Fronts

The observed Salish method of building a three-unit collar begins by working the collar base stitches set aside earlier, or by picking up two neck edge stitches if none were set aside.

COLLAR ON MODERN SWEATER WITH A SHORT COLLAR STAND FOLLOWED BY FLARE CREATED THROUGHOUT THE REMAINDER OF THE COLLAR DEPTH. COURTESY OF NORA GEORGE, WESTHOLME, BRITISH COLUMBIA.

KNITTING TECHNIQUES

INSTRUCTIONS: *Seamless Collar Fronts*

- Attach the yarn at the inside edge of the collar so the tail can easily be worked in and concealed.
  - If working in garter stitch, knit all rows.
  - If working in ribbing, establish the knit-purl sequence so that the outer edge of the collar has a knit stitch on the face of the collar.
- Work collar back and forth, picking up a new stitch each time the neck edge is reached (at the end of every other row). As the pickup occurs only at the neck edge, two rows must be knit for every new stitch.

Note: If the first stitch was slipped on the neck edge, one new stitch will be picked up in every slipped stitch.

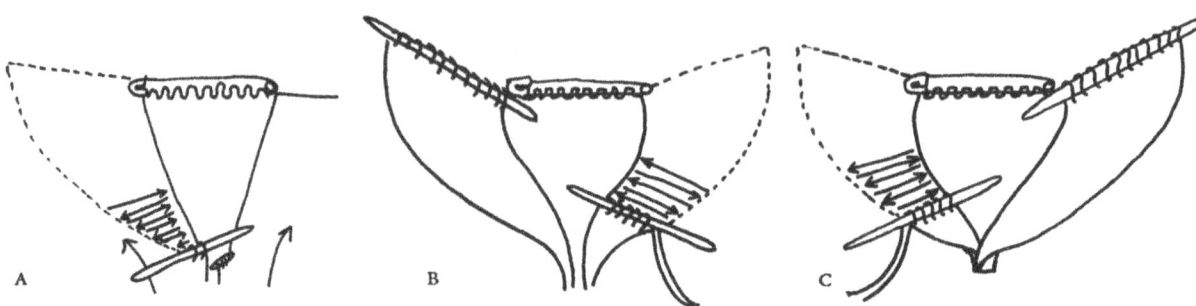

3-UNIT SEAMLESS COLLAR

A. SIDE COLLAR BUILT STARTING WITH 2 BASE STITCHES AND PICKING UP ONE STITCH AT NECK EDGE.
B. PROCESS REPEATED ON SECOND SIDE.
C. FOR PULLOVER, FRONT POINTS OVERLAP.

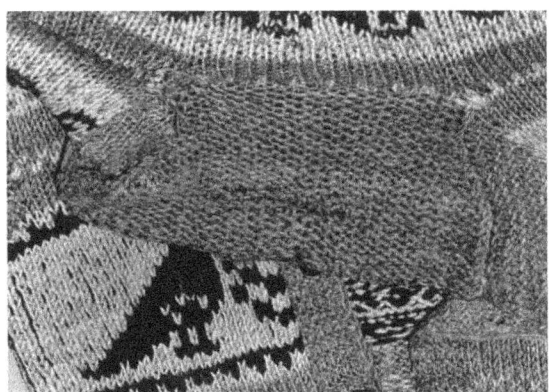

COLLAR ON OLDER SWEATER WITH SHORT COLLAR STAND FOLLOWED BY A SECTION BUILDING FLARE AS STITCHES ARE PICKED UP, BUT NOT JOINED WITH, THE LAST STITCH OF EACH COLLAR FRONT. WHEN MAXIMUM FLARE IS REACHED, STITCHES ARE JOINED, CREATING A SECOND STRAIGHT SECTION. FROM THE COLLECTION OF THE UNIVERSITY OF BRITISH COLUMBIA MUSEUM OF ANTHROPOLOGY, VANCOUVER, BRITISH COLUMBIA.

With the addition of a new stitch at the neck edge every other row, the collar becomes joined invisibly to the sweater and widens as the work progresses upwards.

Wide collars, often eight inches deep at the back, were common on the older sweaters; a six-inch depth is the norm today. The width of the collar is determined by the number of stitches picked up along the neck edge of the sweater front. A shallow V-neck will have a narrower collar.

The width of the collar, even in a deep V-neck, can also be controlled once its desired width is reached, by joining each picked-up stitch with the last stitch at the collar edge, passing the old stitch over the new stitch.

Plain Collar Back

After both collar fronts have been worked up to the shoulder, the work on the collar back commences, leaving the collar front stitches on their respective needles.

Using another needle, the collar back is worked back and forth, adding one stitch from the front collar needles at the end of every row.

INSTRUCTIONS: *Plain Collar Back*

- Using another needle, work the collar back back-and-forth.
- Add one stitch from the collar front needles at the end of every row until all front collar stitches have been incorporated. The back collar is then bound off in pattern (garter stitch or ribbing.)

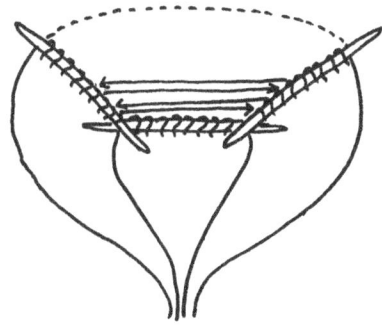

PLAIN COLLAR BACK

BACK NECK STITCHES WORKED BY ADDING ONE STITCH FROM SIDE COLLAR AT END OF EVERY BACK NECK ROW.

Collar Back with Stand

Most knitters build a collar stand on the back collar segment before increasing its width. The height to which the collar rises above the base of the neck is determined by the depth of the collar stand.

If the collar is worked in garter stitch, the knitter does not need to be concerned about the order of the stitches, but if ribbing is used, continuity of the ribbing must be maintained across the collar.

INSTRUCTIONS: *Collar Back with Stand*

- To build the collar stand, join a stitch from each collar front section with the last stitch from the collar back with the appropriate decrease.
- For ribbing, join the two stitches with a P2 tog. at one end and a Sl 1, K1, PSSO at the other.
- For garter stitch, join with K2 tog. at both ends.
- After the collar stand has reached the desired depth, the curve of the collar is created, allowing it to fit the contour of the neck and shoulders.
- Work across the back neck stitches, knitting one new stitch from each side front, in turn. This increases the collar back by one stitch at the end of every row, first from the one side front and then from the other side front.
- Continue in this manner until all the front collar stitches from both sides have been incorporated into the collar back.
- Bind the back collar off in pattern, either in garter stitch or ribbing as established.

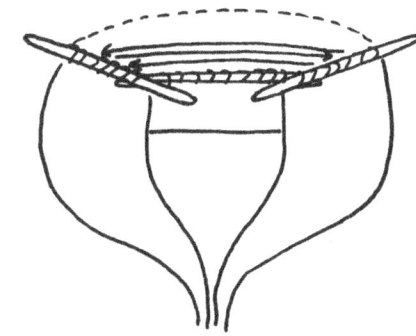

A

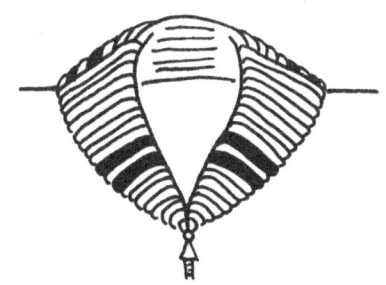

B

COLLAR BACK WITH STAND

A. LAST BACK NECK STITCH JOINED WITH FIRST SIDE COLLAR STITCH AT THE END OF EVERY ROW.
B. FINISHED APPEARANCE OF COLLAR.

KNITTING TECHNIQUES

COLLAR FRONT SECTIONS ARE BOUND OFF AT THE TOP, THE BIND-OFF CREATING A DECORATIVE RIDGE WHERE COLLAR FRONT JOINS COLLAR BACK. NOTE THE TRIPLE BIND-OFF SHOULDER TREATMENT ON THIS SWEATER BY AGNES THORNE.

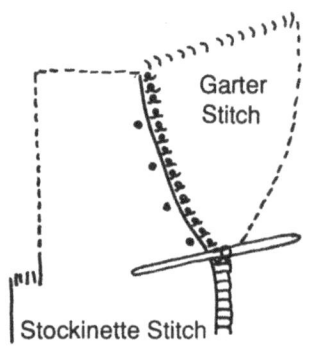

ALTERNATIVE METHOD FOR 3-UNIT COLLAR.

SIDE COLLAR FRONT IS KNIT CONCURRENTLY WITH SIDE FRONT OF SWEATER. SWEATER FRONT IS DECREASED AT REGULAR INTERVALS. COLLAR IS INCREASED ONE STITCH ON EVERY RIGHT-SIDE ROW WHERE IT MEETS SIDE FRONT. COLLAR BACK IS WORKED AS FOR ONE OF THE PREVIOUS COLLAR VARIATIONS.

Alternate Methods of Shaping

A variation in working technique on the three-part collar can be used to establish a visual demarcation between the front and back collar sections. In this case, the knitter binds off across the upper edges on the face of both collar fronts. The collar back is built as before, with one exception. As there are no stitches on either collar front, new stitches must be picked up *behind* the bind-off chain. The bind-off chain thus becomes a decorative feature on the face of the collar. See photo at left.

The collar fronts can also be established concurrently with the garment side fronts with relative ease, but this technique appears to be practiced by only one family of knitters. To do so requires that the pattern stitch of the collar be established at the point desired for the V-neck, increasing one stitch at the neck edge of the collar on every other row while, at the same time, decreasing periodically on the side front to develop the V-shape of the neckline. (See diagram at left.) In the example studied, the decreases for shaping the neck occurred midway between neck edge and armhole edge. The collar back with a stand was the same as previously described.

Continuous Collar

A continuous, one-piece shawl collar was used on the sweaters as early as the 1930s. This style remained popular for a number of years, especially in the 1960s. Recently, it has become less common, with many Salish knitters pressing for a return to the traditional techniques and designs. Many of the older sweaters had horizontal stripes midway up the collar front and across the collar back. The continuous collar does not allow the use of this design element.

This collar is seamless and is worked as a single unit from collar front to collar front around the perimeter of the neck edge. As with the sectional collar, the continuous style is begun with a set of base stitches, although it is often worked from a straight edge by picking up two stitches at the point of the V-neck. This collar can be worked in garter stitch or in a K1, P1 ribbing.

Flare on Front

The collar stand and flare are created by the ingenious use of a short-row technique. Salish knitters do not seem to make special provisions for working these partial rows – they simply turn and continue knitting, even when working across turns of the previous row. Flare is built by working back and forth on the outer collar edge, working one less stitch at the neck edge each time. Flare is built in the reverse direction on the opposite side, working on one more stitch at the neck edge each time.

BELOW: CONTINUOUS COLLAR, FLARE ON FRONT:

A. FLARE IS BUILT BY WORKING SHORT ROWS FROM OUTSIDE EDGE AFTER COLLAR WIDTH IS REACHED.

B. APPEARANCE OF FINISHED COLLAR IN GARTER STITCH.

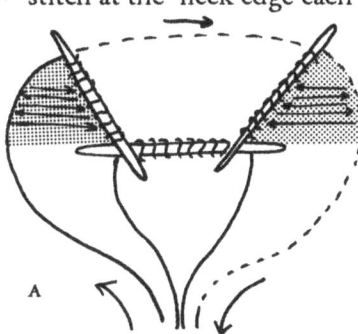

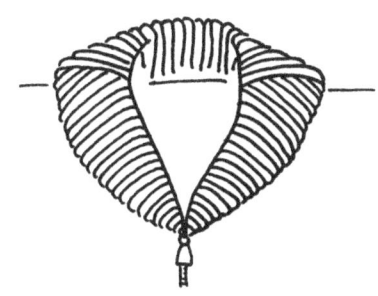

INSTRUCTIONS: *One-Piece Collar, Flare on Front*

- Work the collar back and forth across the stitches, picking up one stitch at the neck edge each row as for the three-part collar. But, rather than ending at collar side front, work across back neck edge.

- When the first shoulder area is reached, knit to within a few stitches of the neck edge. This number of stitches is determined by the depth collar stand desired.

- Turn and work back to the outside edge; then turn and work back to within one stitch of the first turn; turn and work back.

- Continue working short rows, building up the outer portion of the collar, until only two stitches remain at the collar edge.

- Knit the collar back, working across all the stitches on the needle to neck edge.

- Pick up one stitch from the back neck and join it with the last stitch of the collar, passing the collar stitch over the back neck stitch.

- Continue in this manner to second shoulder.

- At the position on opposite side, work a series of short rows in the reverse direction: Work to outer edge, turn and work two stitches back toward the neck edge, turn and work these stitches; turn and work the next row with one more stitch before turning.

- Continue knitting one stitch more on each return toward the neck edge. This builds flare to match that previously developed on the other side of the collar.

- Continue short rows until only the number of stitches required for the collar stand are left unworked. At this point, all stitches of the row are worked and the descent of the side front of the collar begins.

- Working down the neckline, connect collar to neck edge by picking up a stitch from the edge and joining it with the last collar stitch.

- To reduce the number of stitches while descending to the collar base, K2 tog. on every row which begins at the neck edge.

- Continue until the number of stitches remaining on the needles equals the number of the base stitches for the collar.

- Join these center front stitches by grafting or binding off the two sets of stitches together.

- If there were no base stitches, end the collar with a 2 tog., drawing the strand through the final loop.

BELOW: CONTINUOUS COLLAR, FLARE ON BACK

A. SHORT ROWS WORKED FOR FLARE AFTER SIDE FRONTS ARE COMPLETED.
B. FINISHED APPEARANCE OF COLLAR IN GARTER STITCH.

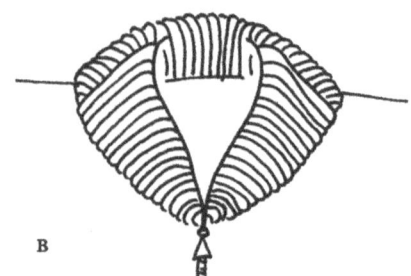

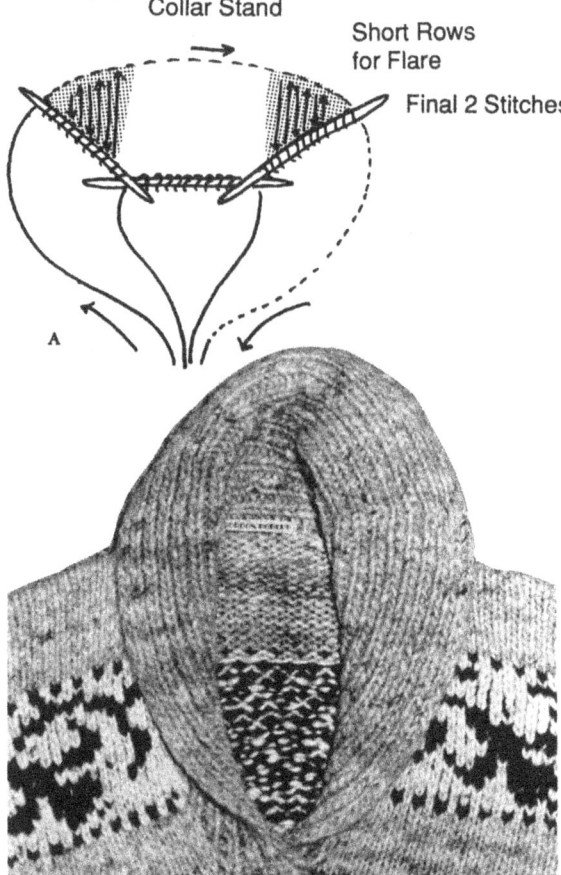

PULLOVER COLLAR OVERLAPS AT THE CENTER FRONT AND IS WORKED IN THE CONTINUOUS ONE-PIECE METHOD IN RIBBING. COURTESY OF DEBBIE WATSON, GEORGETOWN, MASSACHUSETTS.

Sleeves

Flare on Back

The flare on the shoulders can also be established by reversing the order of the two sections described above. When reversed, the flare builds on the collar back. The directional lay of the collar flare is a matter of the knitter's preference. (See illustration below.)

Pullover Collars

Pullover collars are worked in the same manner as the cardigan collars. At the center front, some knitters simply divide the collar base stitches in half and begin the collar. Others prefer to pick up all of the base stitches, overlapping the side collar at center front. This reinforces the point, eliminating the strain that dividing stitches evenly puts on one strand of yarn. With the continuous collar method, all base stitches are picked up on the first side and grafted on the final side. Another reinforcement option is to overlap only one or two stitches from each side to control the stress at the center front.

Traditionally, Salish sweater sleeves were made by picking up stitches around the armhole, beginning with the underarm stitches that were set aside earlier. They were worked down to the cuff, reducing the width below the underarm as necessary, and ended with a band of ribbing at the cuff. On many early sweaters, the decreases occurred around the circumference of the sleeve in the solid heather ground. Most modern sweaters have paired decreases at the underarm.

Today, many knitters prefer to cast on for the band of ribbing and work up towards the shoulder, increasing the width as necessary. The quality of the results of these two methods is the cause of considerable disagreement

SLEEVE OPTIONS

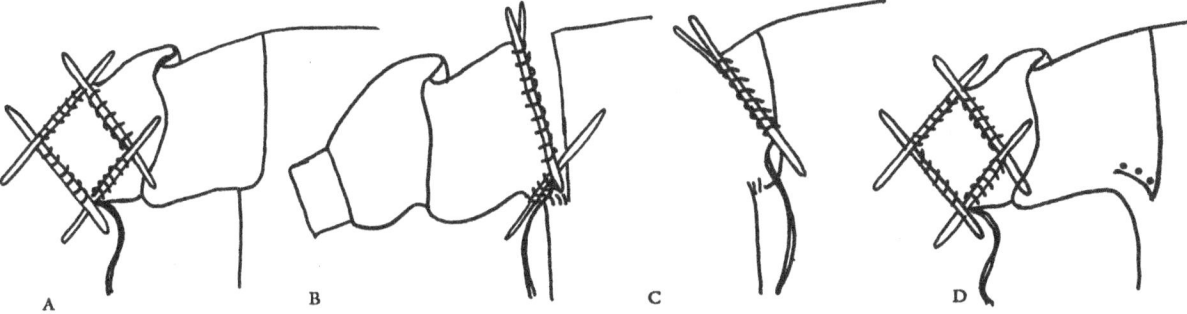

among the Salish knitters. One method is not necessarily of higher quality than the other – the quality of a garment lies in the ability of the knitter to handle the various techniques employed.

A. SLEEVE PICKED UP AND WORKED DOWN.
B. SLEEVE WORKED FROM CUFF UP TO BE GRAFTED INTO OR BOUND OFF INTO ARMHOLE.
C. SHAPED SLEEVE CAP.
D. SLEEVE WITH HALF-GUSSET.

Picking Up Stitches At Armhole

The older method of picking up around the armhole is the simpler method for working a high-quality sleeve, independent of the knitter's skills. There are some disadvantages to this method. The sweater is large and heavy at this point in its construction. An average adult sweater can weigh as much as four pounds. One exceptionally large sweater examined, knit on consignment for a very large person, weighed nearly nine pounds! (See photo, page 28). This is considerable weight for the knitter to maneuver while constructing the sleeve, not to mention that working such a garment in the summer heat would not be pleasurable. Many knitters trying to eke out a living have found that if the sleeves are worked separately, children can help produce the sleeves while the more experienced knitter can concentrate on the more difficult body and collar of the sweater.

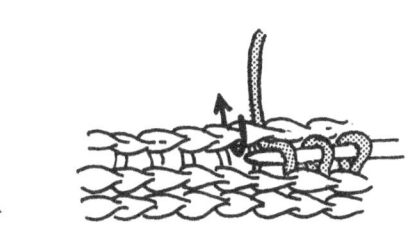

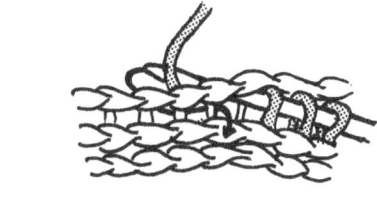

PICKING UP STITCHES AT ARMHOLE EDGE

A. NEEDLE INSERTED FROM FRONT TO BACK BETWEEN LAST 2 ROWS OF ARMHOLE.
B. WORKING YARN BROUGHT THROUGH FROM BACK TO FRONT.

For other knitters, the decision to knit up rather than down is based on design considerations. The design elements of the sweaters are color-stranded. If the sleeve is worked upside down, from the top down to the cuff, the "V" of the knit stitch will be inverted relative to the knit stitches on the body. In the bold designs of the Indian sweater, this reverse effect is noticeable and disconcerting to some consumers. Thus, many knitters have responded by working from the cuff up to the shoulder.

KNITTING TECHNIQUES

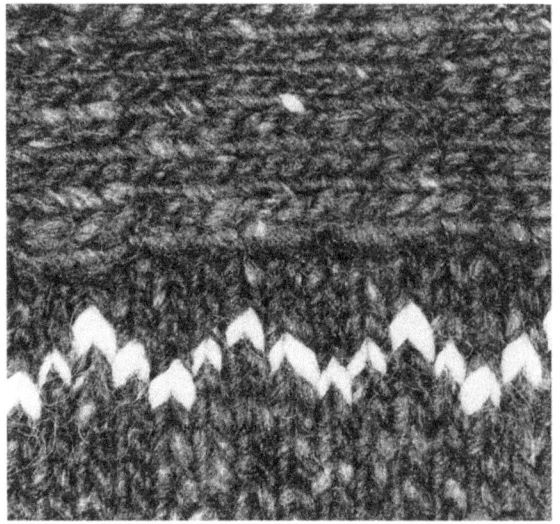

A

B

A. STITCHES PICKED UP AND WORKED DOWN FROM ARMHOLE. THE V OF THE KNIT STITCH IS INVERTED RELATIVE TO THOSE OF THE BODY OF THE SWEATER.

B. WORKING UP FROM THE CUFF AND GRAFTING SLEEVE INTO ARMHOLE. THIS TECHNIQUE ELIMINATES THE INVERTED V OF THE KNIT STITCH RELATIVE TO THOSE OF THE BODY OF THE SWEATER.

Joining A Separate Sleeve To The Body

To successfully join the completed sleeve to the armhole requires skill on the part of the knitter if the garment is going to look good, be comfortable to wear, and be durable. To simply bind off and then sew the sleeve into the armhole is the method most frequently practiced. This method is not very satisfactory as the seam is visually undesirable and quite bulky. And, for many of the Salish, it is too much of a break with tradition, for the garment is no longer seamless.

The more skillful knitters can make the join in one of two ways, either of which, if carefully handled, is of the same quality as the traditional method, while gaining the advantage of less bulk to manage and eliminating the inverted knit stitch in the color-stranded design.

Bind-Off Method

The method most commonly seen in executing a successful join of sleeve to armhole is that of binding off into the armhole; i.e., binding off the underarm stitches together with the corresponding underarm stitches of the sleeve and continuing around the armhole. But, if the knitter is not skillful, such a join is quite literally binding! Control of tension is critical, for if the loops are drawn too tightly in binding off, the armhole will not be comfortable to the wearer.

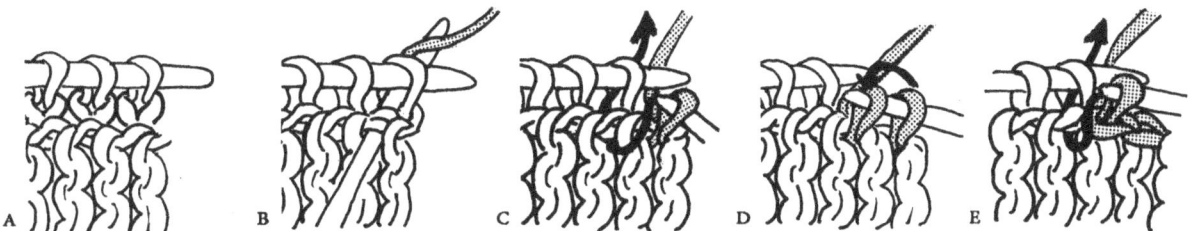

BINDING SLEEVE OFF INTO ARMHOLE

A. SLEEVE PLACED INTO ARMHOLE, RIGHT SIDES TOGETHER. B. WORKING NEEDLE PASSED BETWEEN ROWS TO ENTER FIRST SLEEVE STITCH KNITWISE C. LOOP DRAWN THROUGH STITCH AND THROUGH EDGE OF ARMHOLE BETWEEN ROWS. D. FIRST STITCH BOUND OFF WITH PASS-OVER. E. BIND-OFF CHAIN IN ARMHOLE.

INSTRUCTIONS: *Bind-Off Sleeve Join*

- Divide stitches on three needles, one needle for the underarm stitches, the remainder divided equally on two needles.

- Place sleeve into the armhole, right sides together.

- Bind underarm stitches off together as described for the shoulders:

  Enter the needle through the armhole edge and through the sleeve stitch, drawing a loop through both and continuing the bind-off.

Grafting Method

Another joining method practiced by some more sophisticated Indian knitters, is that of grafting the sleeve into the armhole. This technique appears to have originated among the Salish. As most folk knitters of other cultures worked with finer yarns, grafting would have been rather tedious and, in some cases, detrimental to the yarn. But in the heavy yarns of the Salish, it is very effective. Grafting is not simply whipping the stitch loops down to the armhole, but a totally invisible join. It is the technique used for joining the toe of a stocking.

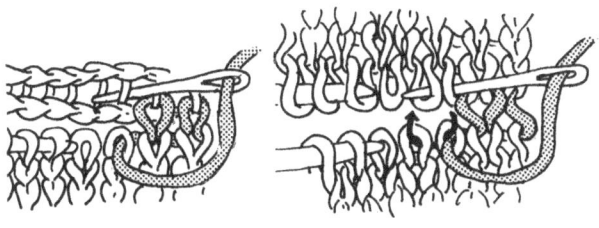

GRAFTING

A. GRAFTING INTO ARMHOLE EDGE.
B. GRAFTING UNDERARM STITCHES.

INSTRUCTIONS: *Grafted Sleeve Join*

- When the sleeve is completed, break off the yarn, leaving a strand long enough to work around the armhole. (4 to 5 times the circumference). Thread the yarn on a large, blunt tapestry needle.

- Divide sleeve stitches onto three needles, the underarm stitches on one and the remainder divided equally on two needles.

- Graft the underarm stitches first. Beginning with the first underarm stitch, lace the yarn through the loops in the same path that it would follow in knitting.

- To begin, enter the first underarm stitch purlwise, then the corresponding sleeve stitch knitwise.

- Reenter the first underarm stitch knitwise, continuing into the second stitch purlwise.

- Reenter the first sleeve stitch purlwise, the second knitwise.

- Repeat the last two steps until all underarm stitches have been joined.

- Continue grafting around the armhole. Each loop must be entered twice – first coming out of the middle of the loop, then passing through the armhole edge, coming back down to reenter the same loop and proceeding to the next loop.

KNITTING TECHNIQUES

To the untrained eye, this join is not discernible from picking up stitches and working down, for there is no bound off edge at the underarm. The only clue that grafting has been used is that the cuff has a cast-on edge and the "V" of the knit stitch in the design is not inverted relative to the stitches on the body of the sweater. But the knitter must be skilled in tensioning the grafting yarn without the aid of a knitting needle.

Shaped Sleeve Cap

Even when picking up the stitches at the armhole and working down, some specialized techniques are practiced by some knitting families. One family of knitters prefers to shape the armhole rather than follow the traditional straight line armhole. This requires the building of a small cap at the upper sleeve if the sweater is to fit properly.

INSTRUCTIONS: *Shaped Sleeve Cap*

- Pick up the center one-third of the stitches at the top of the armhole and purl back.

- Pick up several new stitches purlwise, turn and knit back. Be careful to begin the pick-up at the end of the very first row on the armhole edge. Otherwise, a hole may appear on the sleeve.

- Pick up several new stitches knit wise, turn and purl back.

- Repeat until the entire armhole edge has been worked.

- Add the underarm stitches and work the sleeve in the round down to the cuff.

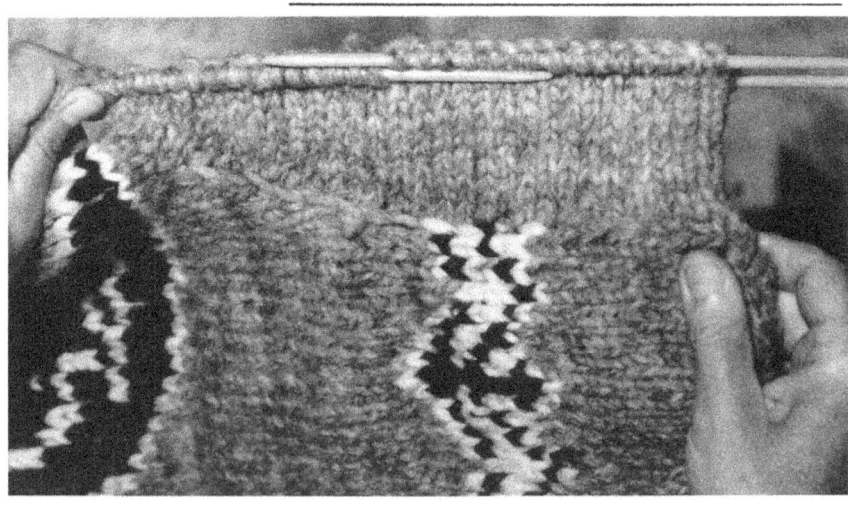

ARMHOLE IN PROGRESS ILLUSTRATING THE SLEEVE CAP PICK-UP USED WHEN THE ARMHOLE IS SHAPED. COURTESY OF NORA GEORGE, WESTHOLME, BRITISH COLUMBIA.

Deep Armhole with Gusset

Another family prefers to make a deeper armhole than usual in order to develop a half-gusset on the sleeve. This additional depth is about 1 1/2 inches or a depth to equal the nine rounds necessary to complete the half-gusset. After the sleeve stitches have been picked up at the armhole, a paired decrease is executed on each side of the underarm stitches on every third round three times. A Sl1, K1, PSSO decrease is used before the underarm stitches, and a K2 tog. decrease is used after the underarm stitches. The deeper armhole greatly increases the maneuverability for the wearer, yet the sleeve is not loose and bulky since the extra depth is removed rapidly.

SWEATER WITH HALF-GUSSET ON THE SLEEVE, A TECHNIQUE INCORPORATED BY MONICA JOE. COURTESTY OF BETTY WHITE'S GIFTS, COWICHAN BAY, BRITISH COLUMBIA.

Obviously, all Indian sweaters are not alike! Rather, the knitters are individual craftspeople, pursuing their work within the time-honored traditions of their families. The techniques are passed from generation to generation, often shared with a neighbor, with the more outstanding knitters building on the work of the preceeding generations. In this way, the tradition keeps pace with the times yet never loses sight of its roots.

These wonderful garments have spawned many commercial "look-alike" patterns for knitters to make in commercially prepared unspun roving-type yarns. They seldom truly capture the spirit of the originals as the designs are more often pictorial than representational and the structure is usually modified with raglan sleeve shaping. And they are sure to have seams!

Some Observations

FRONT AND BACK VIEWS OF A SWEATER MADE BY A HIGHLY TALENTED YOUNGER KNITTER IN 1988, WITH REPRESENTATIONAL DESIGN ON THE BACK, AND COMPLIMENTARY DESIGNS ON THE FRONT. COURTESY OF CLARA CHARLES, WESTHOLME, BRITISH COLUMBIA.

CARDIGAN BY EDITH PAGE, 1988, WITH GEOMETRIC BANDS ABOVE AND BELOW THE DOMINANT BAND, WHICH CONTAINS A SMALL REPRESENTATIONAL BIRD DESIGN. COURTESY OF BETTY WHITE'S GIFTS, COWICHAN BAY, BRITISH COLUMBIA.

The Salish Indian sweater is, by tradition, embellished with color stranded designs. The initial inspiration for this design style may have come from Fair Isle designs worn by the immigrant population. However, once acquainted with Salish textile traditions, one can see that this design embellishment might also be a natural outgrowth of their mastery in the art of weaving both baskets and

CHAPTER SEVEN
The Designs:
Geometric & Representational

blankets before their domination by an alien culture. Regardless of the inspiration, the bold interpretations of the designs and their working techniques have become purely Salish. An interesting aspect of the designs adorning the sweaters is that they apparently have no symbolic significance; they are strictly for ornamentation. Yet every design incorporated into the indigenous weaving is of symbolic importance to the Salish culture.

Working Technique

The Salish use a right-hand manipulation of the yarn when knitting, often referred to as the "English" or "American" style. All colors are worked with the right hand, but the stranding yarn is sometimes manipulated with the left hand while weaving it onto the back surface when not in use for the design. There are no free-floating strands as found in traditional Fair Isle knitting. Fair Isle designs require the use of every color at regular intervals in order to secure them into the fabric. No such restriction is applied to Salish work – the weaving process thus gives them greater freedom in developing designs.

Representational designs, which are not repeated to cover an entire horizontal band are usually worked with color-stranding techniques, weaving the contrast yarn around the body when not in use in the design. When working back and forth, some knitters practice a modified intarsia technique to conserve their

ABOVE: CARDIGAN BY EDITH PAGE, 1988, WITH SWALLOW PATTERN THAT HAS BEEN POPULAR THROUGH THE YEARS. SWEATER HAS BEEN WORKED IN THREE DISTINCT COLORS. COURTESY OF BETTY WHITE'S GIFTS, COWICHAN BAY, BRITISH COLUMBIA.

CARDIGAN SHOWING THAT THE YARN NOT IN USE ON THE SURFACE IS WOVEN IN BETWEEN DESIGN AREAS. COURTESY OF CLARA CHARLES, WESTHOLME, BRITISH COLUMBIA.

COLOR-STRANDED GEOMETRIC PATTERN, THE LOWER BAND WORKED WITH FREE-FLOATING STRANDS IN THE TRADITIONAL FAIR ISLE MANNER AND THE UPPER BAND WORKED WITH WOVEN STRANDS IN THE TRADITIONAL SALISH MANNER. FRONT AND BACK VIEWS.

handspun yarn. Instead of weaving the yarn from one section to another, the contrast-color yarn is woven in for only two or three stitches beyond the design, then it is dropped. Each representational section is worked from a separate ball of yarn. Most of the older knitters do not approve of this modification.

The designs are always worked in natural-colored wools. Some of the wool in the early sweaters was dyed, but the resulting colors were natural in appearance – principally golden brown to reddish browns obtained from natural dye sources. These dyestuffs were later supplemented with purchased packet dyes, the dyes blended to achieve the appearance of the natural colors. In time, the dyed colors were used only to supplement the natural-colored wools when sufficient quantities of the latter could not be secured.

Why the Salish knitters have such a strong affinity for using the natural wool colors cannot be explained. Knitters from families with a multi-generational involvement in knitting all agree that it is simply because the natural colors are more pleasing to the eye. They also report that some knitters had experimented with incorporating other colors, but the results were not satisfactory. Another plausible explanation might be that the use of the natural colors made it possible to incorporate color-stranded designs without the bother of dyeing the wool. Whatever the reasons, today's knitters work only in natural colors, as sufficient supplies are readily available, both from local sources and through imported supplies.

Normally, only two or three colors appear in any one sweater. Most of the older sweaters were worked in three shades. The bands of design were worked in dark wool against white wool. The area between the design bands was worked in a heathered yarn created by blending the dark and white wools in the carding process prior to spinning. This heathered color not only added visual appeal to the garment, but it also served to extend the precious colored fleece. Few knitters today bother with the third heathered color in the sweaters, as it requires carding their own wool, or depending upon the judgment of the custom carder to properly blend the wools. Most knitters now use commerically-prepared rovings in stock colors for their spinning. Therefore, when three colors appear in a sweater today, the result is sharp, and often harsh contrast rather than the cohesive harmony characteristic of the older garments.

A few knitters today are experimenting with the use of a third color in their representational designs. The goal is not to alter the style to the extent that it becomes a pictorial design, but rather to emphasize the design with outlining or by accenting some critical element of the design. Examples include the beaver design as interpreted in three colors by Nora George (see photo, page 20), the raven on the back cover, and the example at right. This type of design enrichment is practiced by very few knitters, for it greatly reduces the speed of knitting.

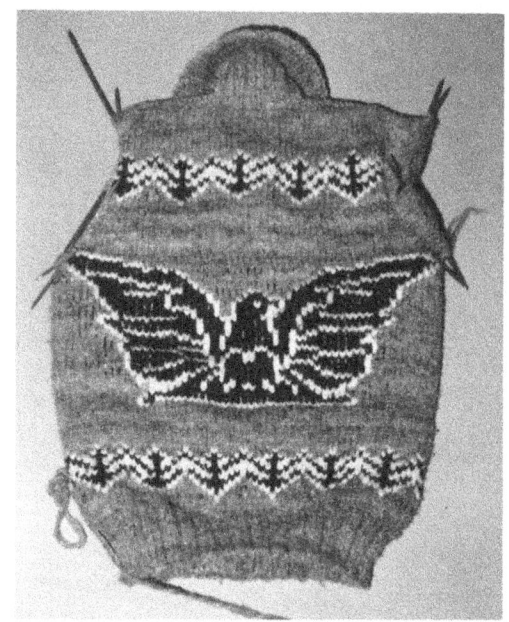

EFFECTIVE USE OF A THIRD COLOR TO ENHANCE A REPRESENTATIONAL DESIGN. SWEATER IN PROGRESS BY NORA GEORGE.

Design Sources

Many early designs preferred by the Salish, both geometric and simple representational motifs, had their roots in the designs utilized previously in their basketry. These designs were easily adapted to their knitting, for certain geometric designs are in universal use in almost any textile technique. Other geometric designs came from the immigrants in the form of printed patterns for knitting, embroidery and the like. As the Indian knitters' expertise grew, they added representational designs to their repertoire.

Early representational designs were usually small, and could be substituted for a geometric band without disturbing the overall pattern sequence. The inspiration for these designs came initially from the world around them: familiar flora and fauna, such as a maple leaf, a swallow, a butterfly. As time passed, larger motifs were incorporated, including the still-popular eagles, whales, deer, and trees. The repertoire continued to expand, eventually including designs from the European culture with which they were surrounded, such as the popular horse motifs, roses and peacocks. Everything became a source for design: the "Congoleum™ pattern" was taken from a popular border design used in linoleum floor covering. The dragon on a

SWEATER IN TWO COLORS WITH O X O PATTERN INCLUDED IN THE TRADITIONAL FORMULA FOR FIVE BANDS OF DESIGN. THE O X O PATTERN IS A POPULAR DESIGN USED IN KNITWEAR FROM MANY CULTURES OF THE WORLD. COURTESY OF BETTY WHITE'S GIFTS, COWICHAN BAY, BRITISH COLUMBIA.

POPULAR O X O PATTERN INTERPRETED IN FOUR COLORS: WHITE, BLACK AND TWO SHADES OF GRAY, 1986. COURTESY OF BETTY WHITE'S GIFTS, COWICHAN BAY, BRITISH COLUMBIA.

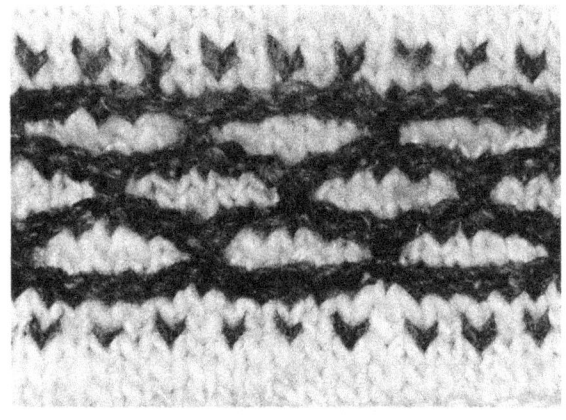

THE ONLY RECORDED TEXTURED DESIGN USED TRADITIONALLY IN THE INDIAN SWEATERS. THE DESIGN ELEMENT IS SIMPLE, USING A PURL ROW AND A SLIP STITCH SEQUENCE IN THE CONTRAST COLOR.

Samplers

tin soon graced an Indian sweater, the eagle on a beer bottle lable found itself perched on a sweater back. Other inspirations came from from Indian art objects such as pictographs and totem poles.

There is always the exception to the rule. One traditional design is not worked by color-stranding. This particular design was first recorded on the Koksilah Reserve in the 1940s and remains popular today. It bears a strong resemblance to a basketry technique and is created with a purl round, slip stitch move.

There are normally three slip stitch sections, beginning and ending with a knit round-purl round in contrast color. The design is usually repeated in all the horizontal bands of the sweater.

INSTRUCTIONS: *Slip Stitch Pattern*

- Knit one round, purl one round, both in the contrast color.
- With main color, knit the next two rounds, slipping every fifth stitch (contrast color).
- With contrast color, knit the next round, continuing to slip fifth stitch as established. This round can be knit without slipping the fifth stitch, but this does not draw the purl together as snugly, so it loses depth.
- Purl one round in the contrast color.
- Knit 2 rounds with main color, slipping every fifth stitch (contrast color), and alternating the sequence to place the slipped stitch midway between those slipped earlier.

Knitted samplers were common among the earliest Indian knitters. Many of today's knitters reminisce about a grandmother's fine sampler, often a long tube of knitting recording her favorite geometric pattern bands and representational designs such as the maple leaf, a butterfly, or a swan. Others describe their elder's cache of patterns worked out on graph paper, often tucked under a mattress for safe keeping! One knitter laments the loss of her mother's magnificent horse pattern which was destroyed in a house fire.

Even today, the patterns of many of the older knitters are still recorded by working them into sample squares, while younger ones prefer to chart their designs on graph paper. Others readily utilize the abundance of printed patterns available to knitters today – some of which are commerical adaptations of earlier Indian designs! Some knitters jealously guard their designs, and even claim proprietary rights in a few cases, while others freely share their design sources.

Regardless of the source, designs utilized by the Salish knitters have a distinctly Indian quality when interpreted into their knitted garments. They are bold in appearance, simplified to bare essentials in order to fit the bulky yarns used for the sweaters. Many knitters who work only on commission design sweaters to suit any fancy. These design may have no native connotations, yet the resulting sweater will have a special aura of "Indian-ness" about it. The handspun yarn and sweater structure lend to this aura, but the knitter's eye for representative design is surely the principal factor. One has but to look at the crude pictorial designs on commercially-made imitations to realize that this aspect of "Indian-ness" is easily compromised.

CARDIGAN BY HARRIET PAIGE, 1988, IN TRADITIONAL DESIGN WITH FIVE BANDS, WORKED IN THREE DISTINCT COLORS TYPICAL OF THE CURRENT ERA. COURTESY OF BETTY WHITE'S GIFTS, COWICHAN BAY, BRITISH COLUMBIA.

Design Placement

The designs appear on the garment in horizontal bands. Early sweaters are usually described as having five bands of design on an adult's sweater. These bands, beginning at the base of the sweater are: (1) a stripe or stripes knitted into the ribbing, (2) a geometric band of moderate proportions, (3) the dominant band, which might be a representational design or a large geometric, (4) a repeat of the second geometric band, and (5) a stripe or stripes in the collar. (Lane, 1951.) The sleeves repeat these designs, with stripes in the ribbing followed by the geometric band of moderate proportions and completed with the large geometric at the upper arm. See illustrations, page 108, 109. If a representational design was used in place of a large geometric on the body, a complimentary design, either representational or geometric, might be used, or the first geometric band repeated on the sleeve.

SWEATER IN THREE COLORS WITH THREE BANDS OF GEOMETRIC DESIGN AND STRIPE IN RIBBING. COURTESY OF BETTY WHITE'S GIFTS, COWICHAN BAY, BRITISH COLUMBIA.

FRONT AND BACK VIEWS OF A 1986 CARDIGAN IN WORKED IN TWO COLORS WITH A LARGE EAGLE ON BACK, TWO SIMILAR BUT SMALLER EAGLES ON FRONT. THE SAME DESIGN, STILL SMALLER, IS CARRIED OUT ON THE UPPER SLEEVES. COURTESY OF BETTY WHITE'S GIFTS, COWICHAN BAY, BRITISH COLUMBIA.

Charts

When representational designs are utilized on a sweater, the front and back of the garment are not always the same. The back often had a single large motif dominating the space. This is repeated on the front if the sweater is a pullover. In the case of a cardigan, the two sides would be mirror images, with some aspect of the back design repeated, or a complimentary design developed for the front. (See photo, page 72.) For instance, if two horses are used on the back, one in profile and one a frontal view, only the frontal view might appear on the cardigan side fronts. Or, if two deer are facing a tree on the back, only the tree might be put on the side fronts.

Children's sweaters often have three bands on the body, all identical and of moderate proportions, similar to the second and fourth bands on the adult sweater. Most children's sweaters contain only small representational designs as the space is too limited for large pattern motifs.

These, of course, are only generalized principles for the design placement – the sweaters were made by individual craftspeople, free to interpret the work as they so desired.

Today's sweaters do not always fit neatly into the early design "formula." Stripes in ribbings and collars were discontinued during the 1960s and 70s, although the striping has become popular once again as knitters are encouraged to maintain the old traditions.

With the absence of the heathered yarn, the very distinctive banding has been altered; bands are still used, but there is no longer a heathered ground and a separate ground color in the design band, unless a third distinct color is used. The continued use of a simple border stripe above and below the geometric bands (often no more than alternate stitches in the two colors), helps to maintain the illusion of separate bands in the two-color sweaters.

Many examples of designs preferred through the years by the Salish knitters follow, including both geometric and representational designs. Most were taken directly from sweaters, some from photographs, and others shared by the knitters. Every attempt has been made to accurately present authentic Indian designs.

This does not mean that all of the designs are original Salish work, although many are. It only infers that these designs have been favored by Salish knitters in the past and/or are in current use, regardless of their origins. A particular design might have several variations, the result of copying another knitter's design without benefit of her chart or sampler, or perhaps as a refinement of another knitter's original design.

This compilation of designs is fairly complete, covering many popular styles. Some of the motifs are very common, others are rarely seen. Regretfully, many old designs have been lost, as no records were kept. Resurrecting them from old photographs has limitations if accuracy is desired.

Many one-of-a-kind designs developed by commission knitters are not included here. Some of the more unusual ones include a fanciful totem replete with tassels, a rendition on special order of a pair of sweaters depicting the old Stone Church (now the Cowichan Band Cultural Center), Duncan, B.C.; and a glorious vining rose whose blossoms entwine body and sleeves.

Border Designs (page 81)

Many geometric bands have a patterned border added above and below the design band. This edging may be in the design color or in the ground color within the design band. In the latter case, the result is a serrated edging rather than a distinct border. These borders are usually two or three-row geometrics, paired above and below the design band. Most are paired as a mirror image; a few are not. In some cases, these borders touch the geometric band and are worked in the design color, thus appearing as an extension of the band.

Geometric Designs (page 82-89)

Geometric bands are typically placed above and below the dominant design. They are more complex than the border designs and usually range in size from four to nine rows in depth. The various small wave patterns are directional, with a distinct upper and lower side. These are often used as mirror images above and below a representational design.

Key to symbols

In the charts that follow, all designs are worked in only two colors unless otherwise noted. In a few cases, slip stitches are employed to add design interest – these are denoted with an "S" on the chart.

THE DESIGNS

Large Geometric Bands

These wide geometric bands, pages 85-86, are typically used as the dominant design in the central position on the sweater. They range in size from ten to twenty rows in depth.

O-X-O Motifs

The O-X-O bands, page 86, are popular in many parts of the world. Salish knitters probably adopted these designs from the Scottish settlers in the region, for they are commonly used in Fair Isle knitting. Their origins are believed to be in the Baltic States.

Geometric Motifs

Geometric motifs, pages 84, 85, 87, are often used in pattern bands, replacing the interconnected geometric borders on page 81. Motifs are evenly spaced according to the number of stitches in the circumference of the sweater. The larger motifs may also be used in conjuction with a large representational design. In this case, the main design is used on the back of the sweater and the smaller motifs are used on each side front of a cardigan.

Representational Bands (page 88)

Many Salish knitters like to use designs from nature. Both leaves and flowers are very popular in pattern bands. Many of the designs do not depict the native flora, but rather are representations of the more exotic plants imported by the European settlers. These designs are very dramatic in appearance when knit in bulky yarns.

Representational Motifs (pages 91-106)

Early representational motifs were small, and placed in borders in lieu of geometric bands. Later, large motifs were incorporated into the sweaters. When large motifs are used, they replace the center design band entirely. Often, the back of a cardigan will have one large design, while the front has two complimentary designs placed as mirror images.

Border Designs

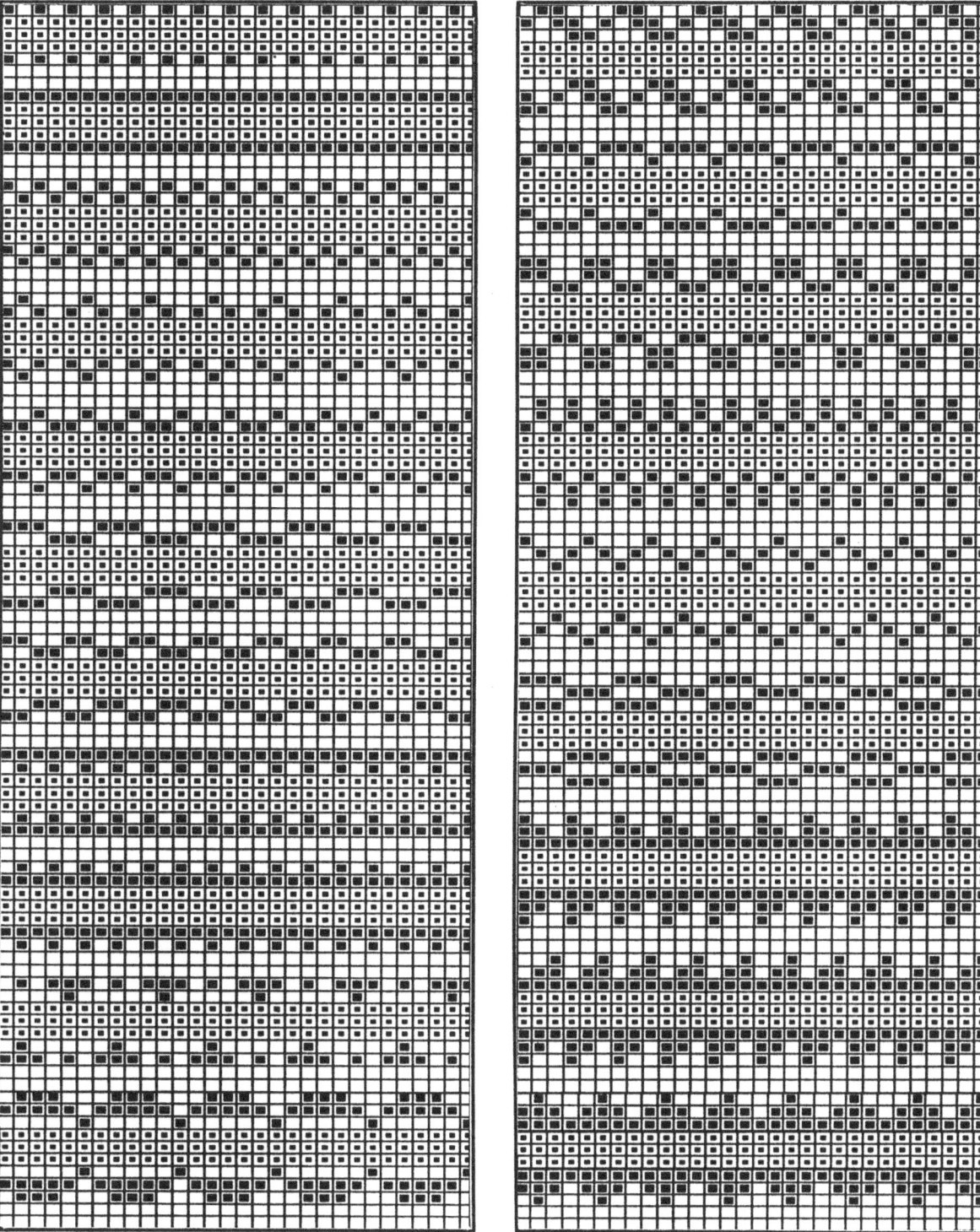

IN THESE BORDER CHARTS (THIS PAGE ONLY) THE SMALL DOT DESIGNATES THE AREA TO BE WORKED WITH A MODERATE-SIZED GEOMETRIC BAND BETWEEN THE TWO PARTS OF THE BORDER MOTIF.

THE DESIGNS

Small Geometric Bands

Moderate-sized Geometric Bands

THESE MOTIFS MAY BE USED IN COMBINATION WITH SMALL BORDER DESIGN.

Large Geometric Bands

NOTE: THESE BANDS ARE EXPANDED VERSIONS OF THE LAST FOUR ON PREVIOUS PAGE. WHEN A LARGE REPRESENTATIONAL DESIGN IS USED, FLANKED WITH THESE SMALL BANDS, THE EXPANDED VERSION APPEARS ON UPPER ARM, THE SMALLER VERSION ABOVE THE WRISTBAND.

Large Geometric Motif

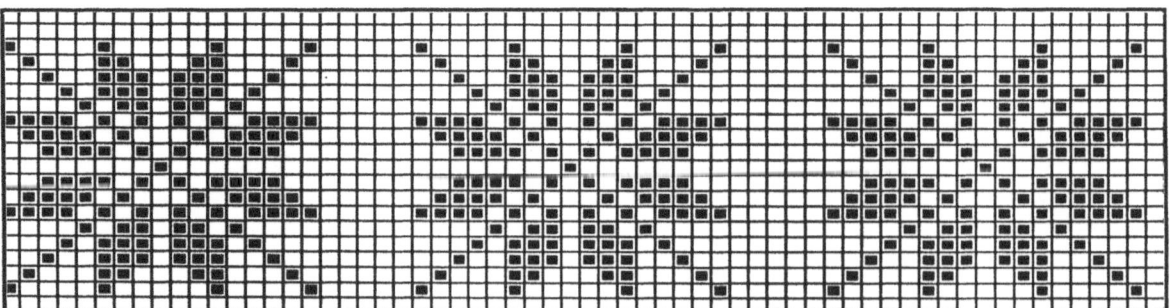

Large Geometric Bands

Large Geometric Motif

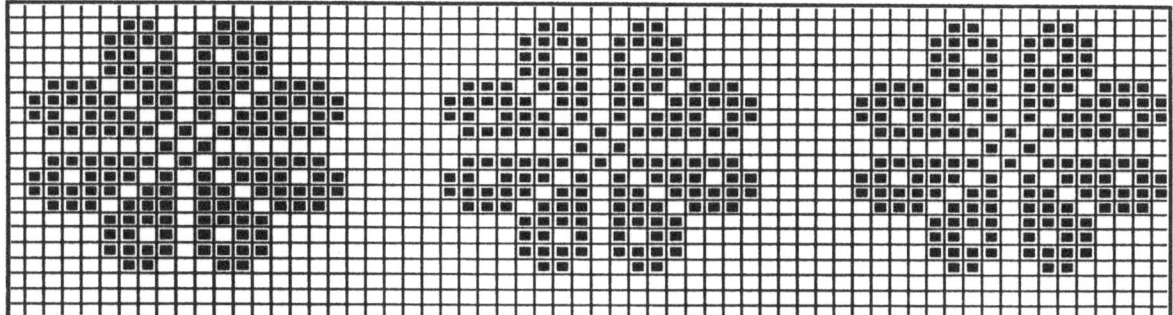

Large Geometric Bands *(continued)*

OXO Bands

Small Geometric Motifs bottom row: Large Geometric Motif.

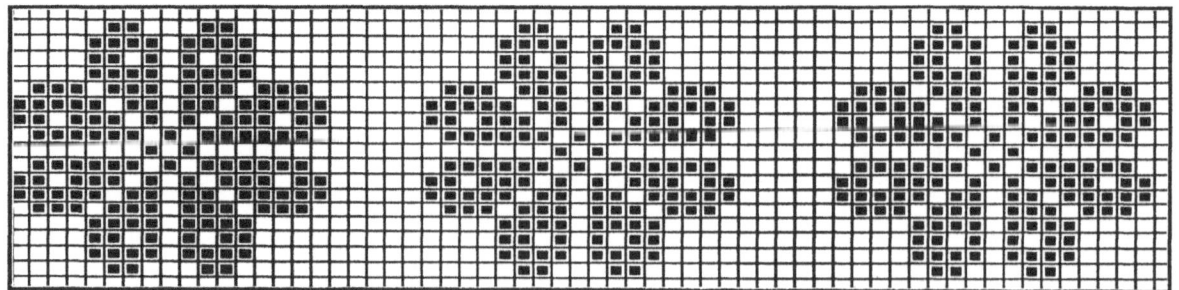

REPRESENTATIONAL BANDS

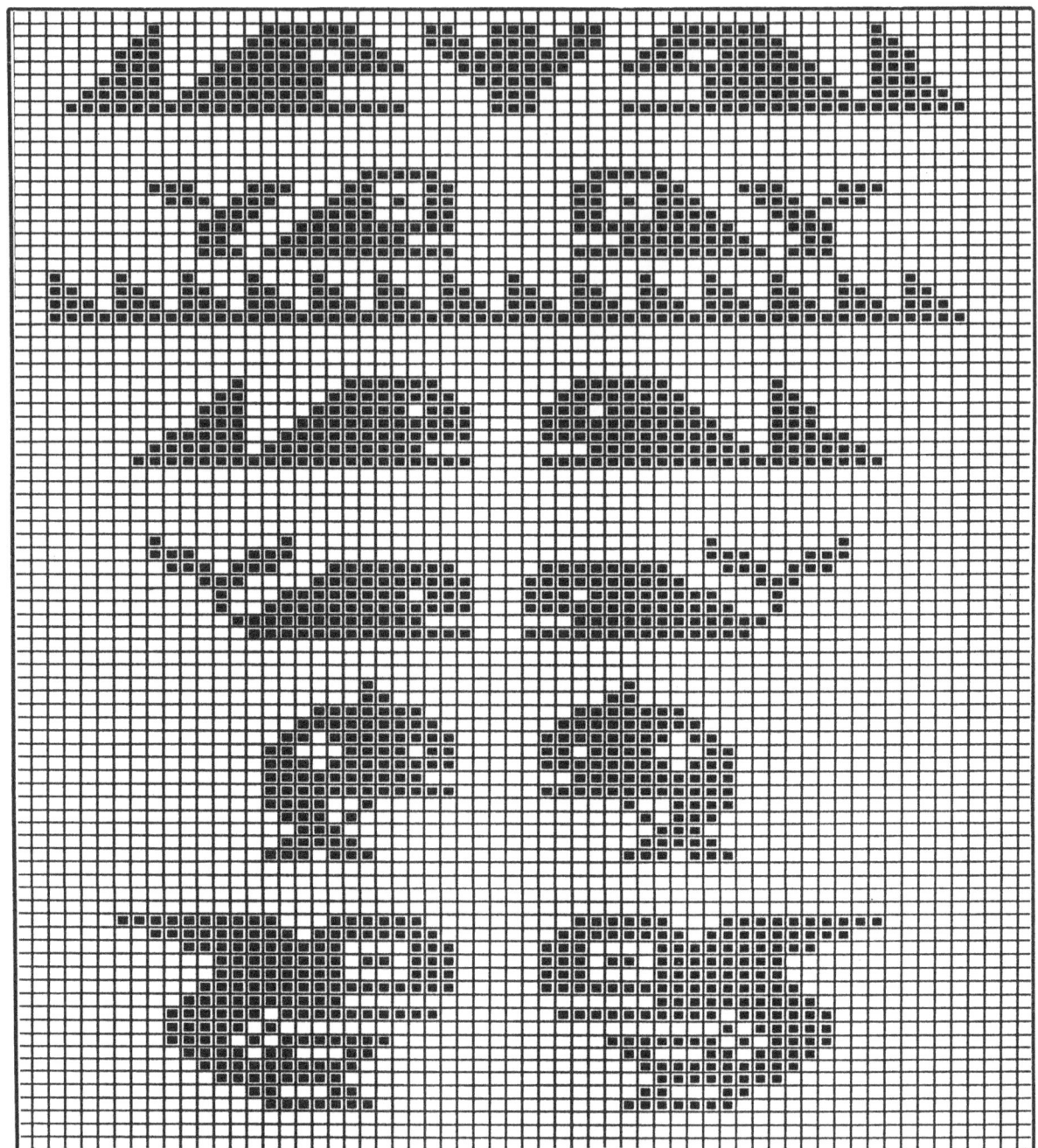

VARIOUS WHALES. THESE ARE VERY POPULAR PATTERNS. SIMILAR DESIGNS APPEARED IN BASKETS OF THE REGION. BOTTOM ROW: KILLER WHALES.

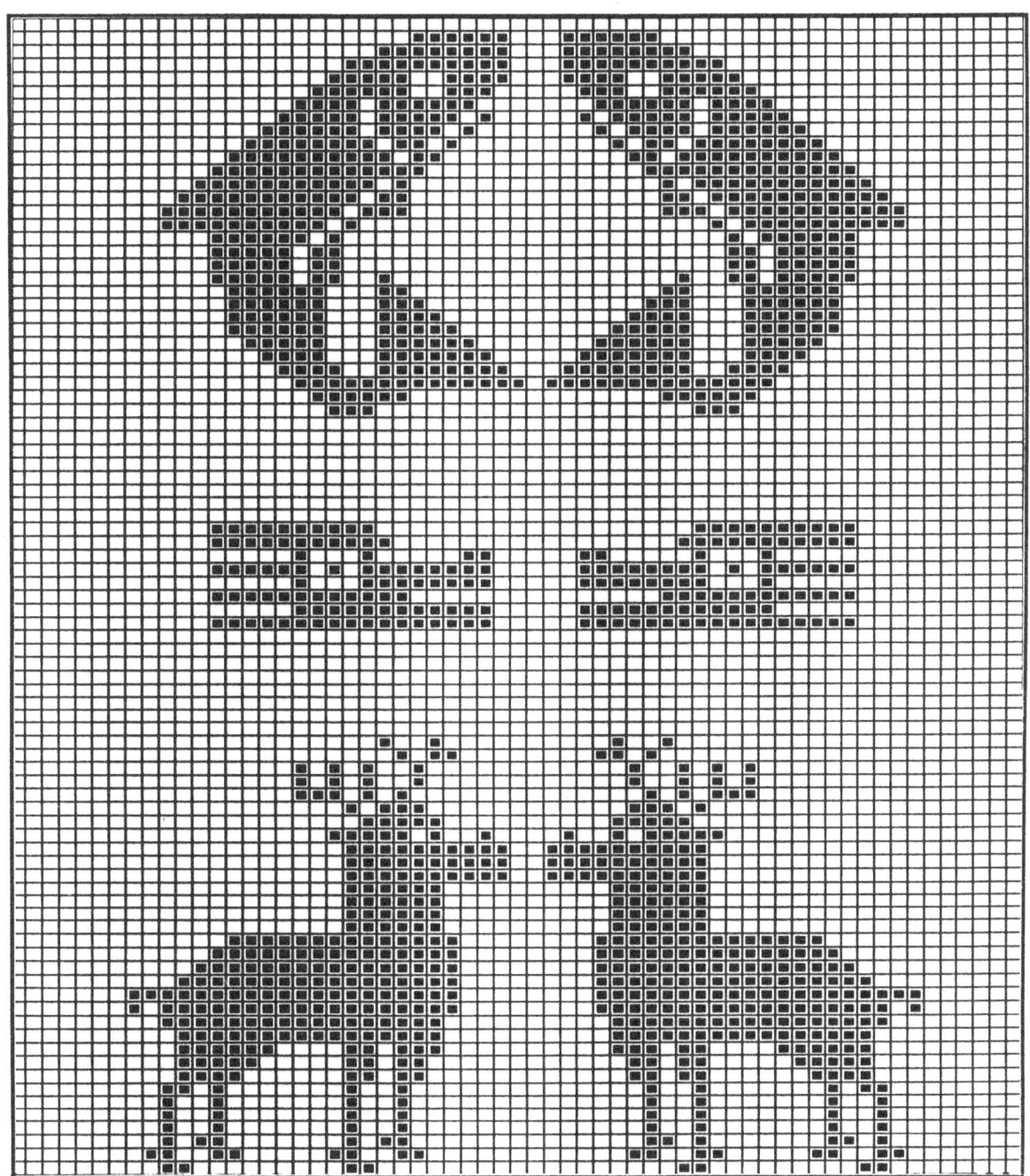

STYLIZED SALMON (TOP) AND MOOSE (BOTTOM). CENTER: WOLF MASK MOTIF.

DEER MOTIFS. TOP: ONE OF THE OLDEST INDIAN PATTERNS THAT HAS BEEN IN CONSTANT USE THROUGHOUT THE YEARS. CENTER: A MODERN VERSION OF THE OLDER DEER DESIGN. BOTTOM: LEAPING DEER.

REPRESENTATIONAL MOTIFS

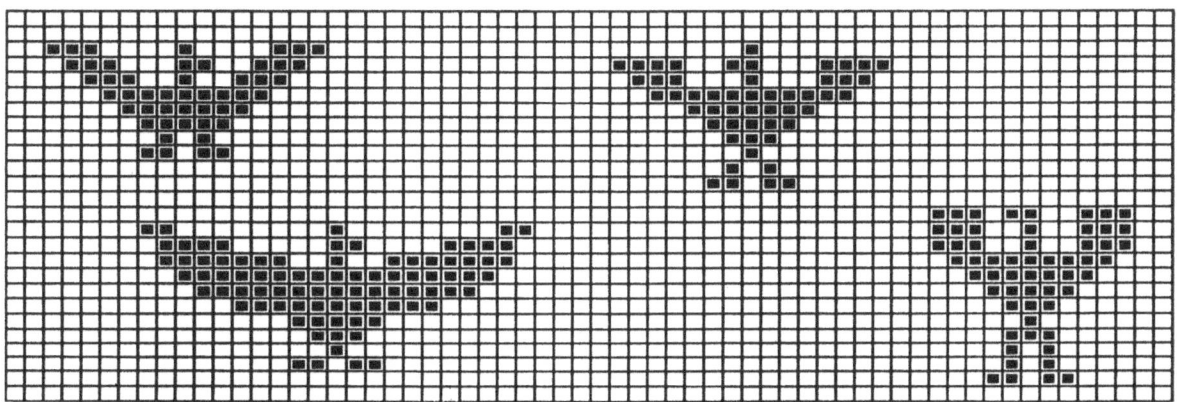

THUNDERBIRDS. THESE EVER-POPULAR MOTIFS ARE OFTEN USED ON CHILDRENS' SWEATERS.

LOWER CHARTS, CLOCKWISE: LOVE KNOT; CAT; HONEYBEE (DESIGN NOT IN CURRENT USE); BUTTERFLY. BOTTOM ROW: MAPLE LEAF DESIGN SAID TO BE ONE OF THE EARLIEST REPRESENTATIONAL DESIGNS. THE VERSION AT LEFT IS OLDER AND WAS RECORDED IN A SAMPLER WHILE THE KNITTER STUDIED A MAPLE LEAF.

THE DESIGNS

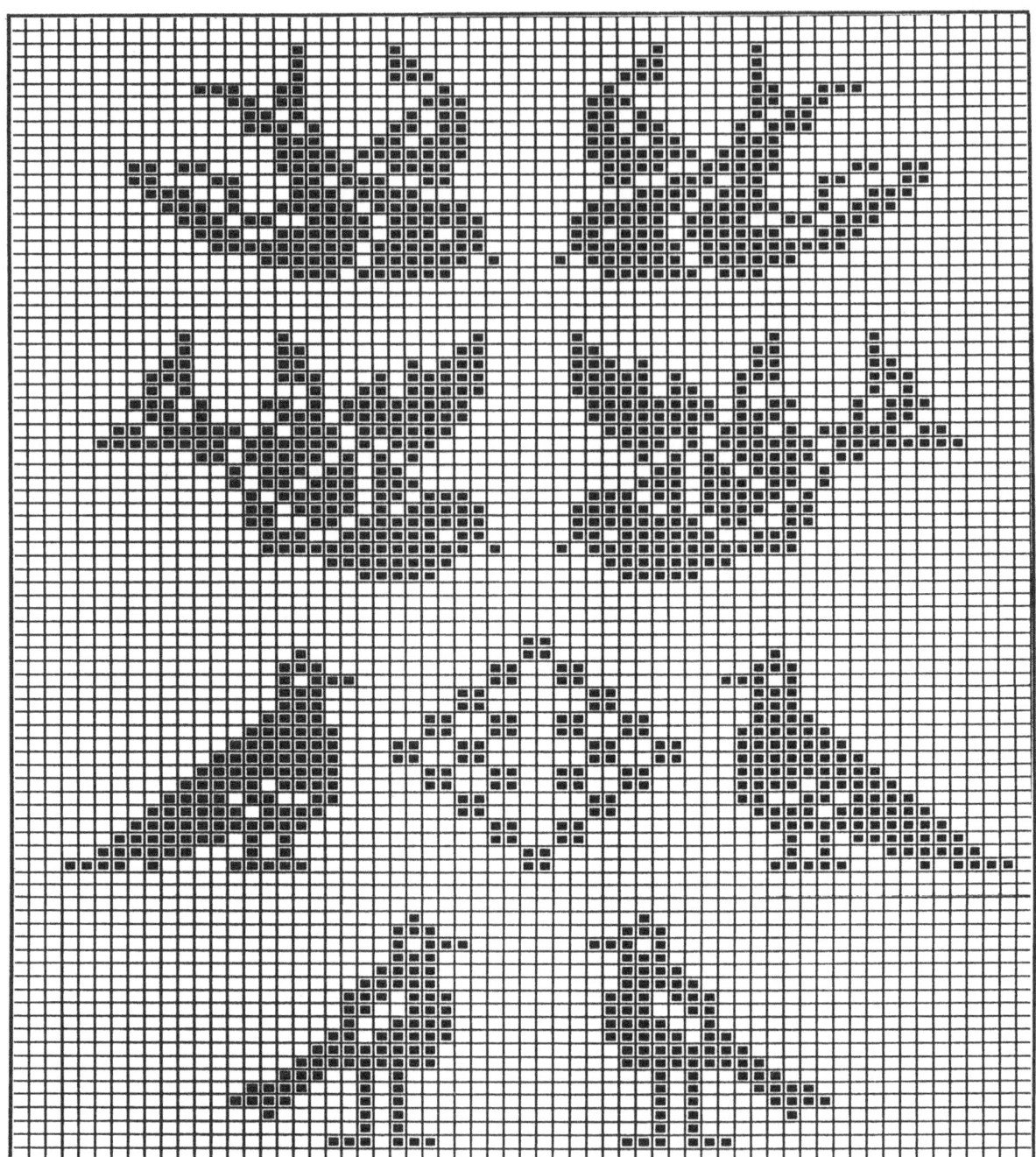

BIRD MOTIFS. TOP: SWALLOW PATTERN POPULAR SINCE THE EARLY 1920S. SECOND ROW: SMALL BIRDS, PROBABLY FROM 1950-60. THIRD AND FOURTH ROWS: TWO OLDER STYLIZED BIRD PATTERNS SELDOM SEEN TODAY.

TOP: BLUE JAY PATTERN THAT WAS POLULAR FROM 1930-1950. THIS PATTERN IS NO LONGER IN COMMON USE WITH TODAY'S BULKY YARNS, FOR IT REQUIRES MANY STITCHES TO COMPLETE ITS WIDTH. CENTER: ADAPTATION OF THE BLUE JAY FOR MODERN BULKY YARNS. FEWER STITCHES ARE REQUIRED. BOTTOM: SHORE BIRDS. THIS PATTERN DOES NOT APPEAR TO BE IN CURRENT USE.

THIS EAGLE CAME FROM A SWEATER BELIEVED TO HAVE BEEN PURCHASED IN THE LATE 1930S OR EARLY 1940S. THIS IMMENSE DESIGN REQUIRES A LARGE NUMBER OF STITCHES AND IS NOT FEASIBLE IN THE BULKY YARNS POPULAR TODAY. IT WAS KNIT WITH 5 STITCHES TO THE INCH.

TOP: SEA MONSTER OR DRAGON PATTERN PRESUMED TO HAVE BEEN TAKEN FROM A CHINESE TEA CANNISTER. CENTER: MYTHICAL SEA MONSTER USED IN THE 1940S. IT DOES NOT APPEAR TO BE IN USE TODAY. PATTERN WAS TAKEN FROM A POOR-QUALITY PHOTOGRAPH AND MAY NOT BE ABSOLUTELY ACCURATE. BOTTOM: SQUIRRELS, TYPICAL OF MANY EARLY REPRESENTATIONAL ANIMAL DESIGNS. THIS PATTERN WAS ALSO TAKEN FROM A POOR-QUALITY PHOTOGRAPH AND MAY NOT BE ACCURATELY REPRODUCED.

THE DESIGNS

EAGLE MOTIFS. THE WIDE SPAN IS SUITABLE FOR PULLOVERS OR CARDIGAN BACKS.

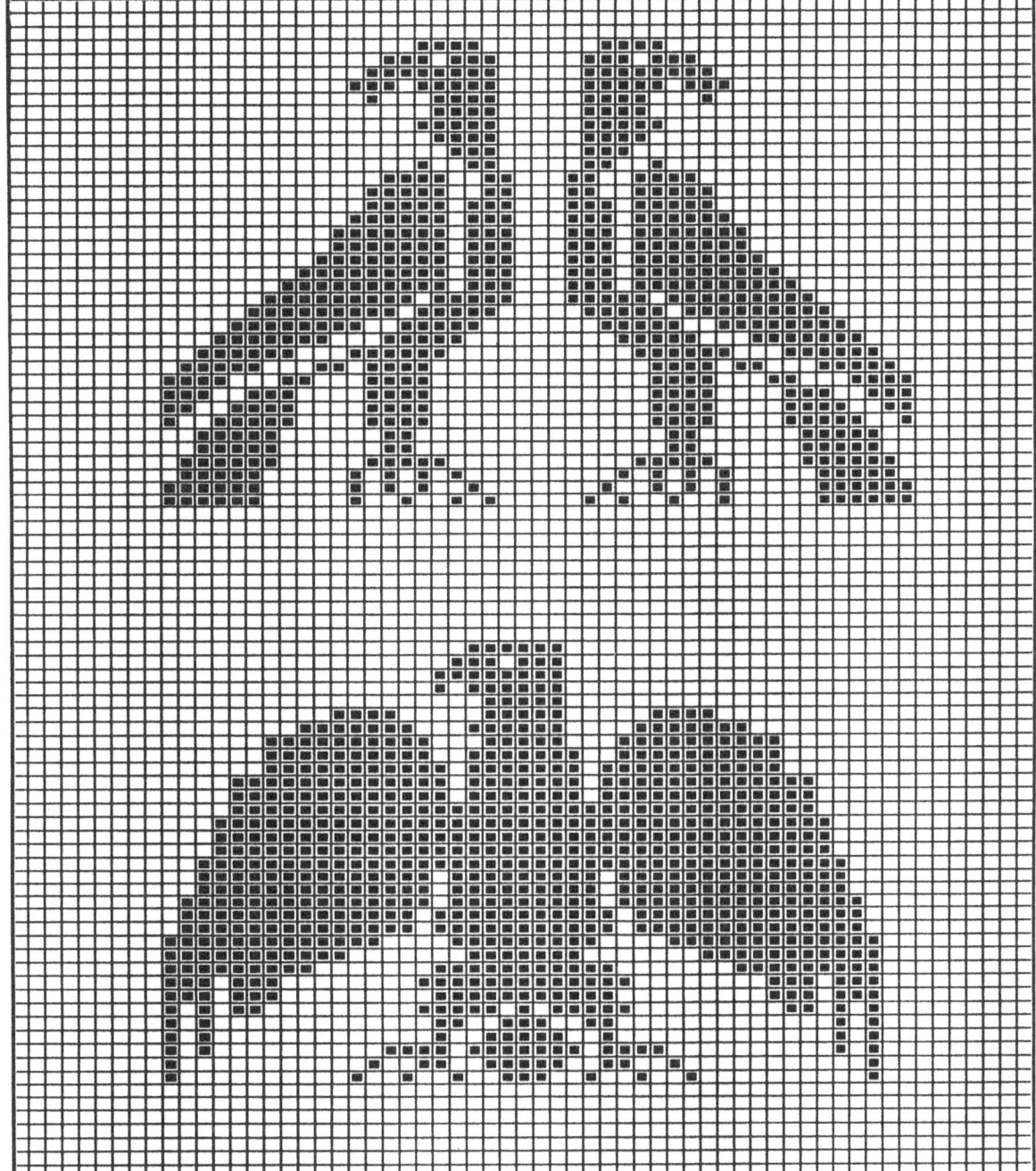

EAGLE MOTIFS.

THUNDERBIRDS AND EAGLES. MANY VERSIONS AND SIZES. A LARGE ONE OFTEN APPEARS ON THE BACK, WITH A SMALLER ONE ON EACH CARDIGAN SIDE FRONT. ANOTHER SMALLER VERSION IS USED ON THE UPPER SLEEVE.

LARGE THUNDERBIRDS. LOWER VERSION HAS SLIP STITCHES INCORPORATED IN THE WINGS TO CARRY THE COLOR OVER TWO ROWS. THIS TENDS TO DRAW THE DESIGN IN, GIVING IT AN INTERESTING TEXTURE. THIS TECHNIQUE APPEARS TO HAVE ORIGINATED WITH THE KNITTERS ON THE KOKSILAH RESERVE, WHERE A TEXTURED DESIGN EMPLOYING PURL STITCHES HAS LONG BEEN POPULAR.

ABOVE AND OPPOSITE: TWO VERSIONS OF TOTEM POLE MOTIF. WHEN USED ON A CARDIGAN, THE FULL TOTEM IS USED ON THE BACK. THE CENTER PORTION WITHOUT THE WING SPAN APPEARS ON EACH SIDE FRONT. ONE SEGMENT, SUCH AS THE CENTRAL OWL FIGURE IS USED ON THE UPPER SLEEVES.

THE DESIGNS 103

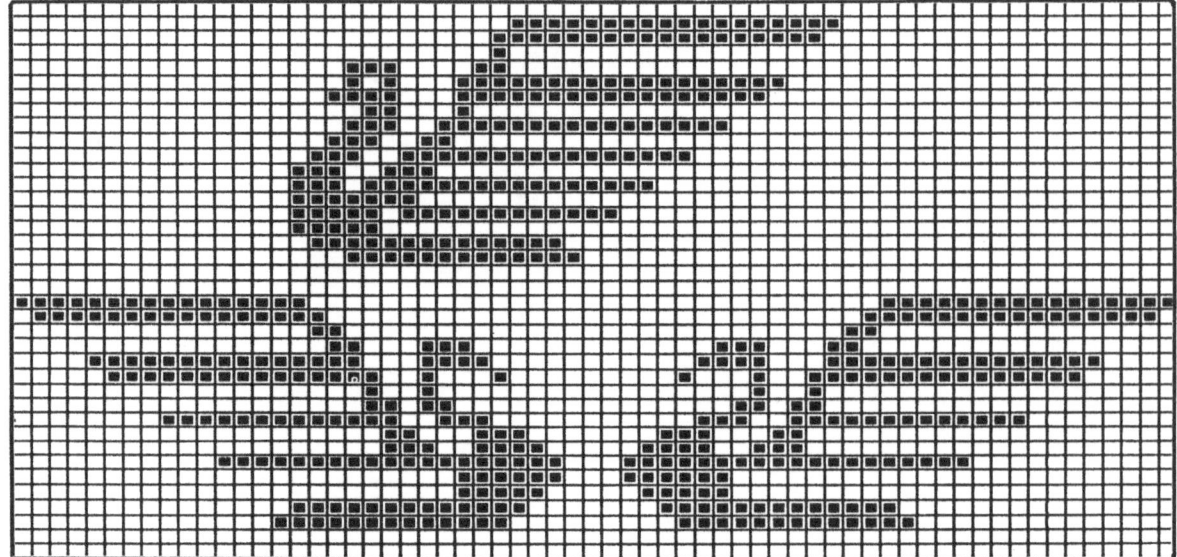

SWAN MOTIF POPULAR ON THE MAINLAND. THE UPPER SWAN IS USED ON A CARDIGAN BACK WITH THE SLIGHTLY SMALLER, LESS BOLD SWANS ON THE FRONT AND UPPER SLEEVES.

HORSE DESIGN TAKEN FROM A SWEATER MADE IN THE 1940S. IT DOES NOT APPEAR TO BE IN USE TODAY. AT LEAST TWO MORE VARIATIONS OF THE HORSE DESIGN HAVE BEEN USED BY INDIAN KNITTERS. ONE VERSION WAS LOST IN A HOUSE FIRE. THE OTHER IS STILL IN USE BUT MORE CLOSELY RESEMBLES A MULE THAN A HORSE. THE PAIR IS USED ON THE BACK WITH ONLY THE HORSE IN THE FOREGROUND IN FRONT.

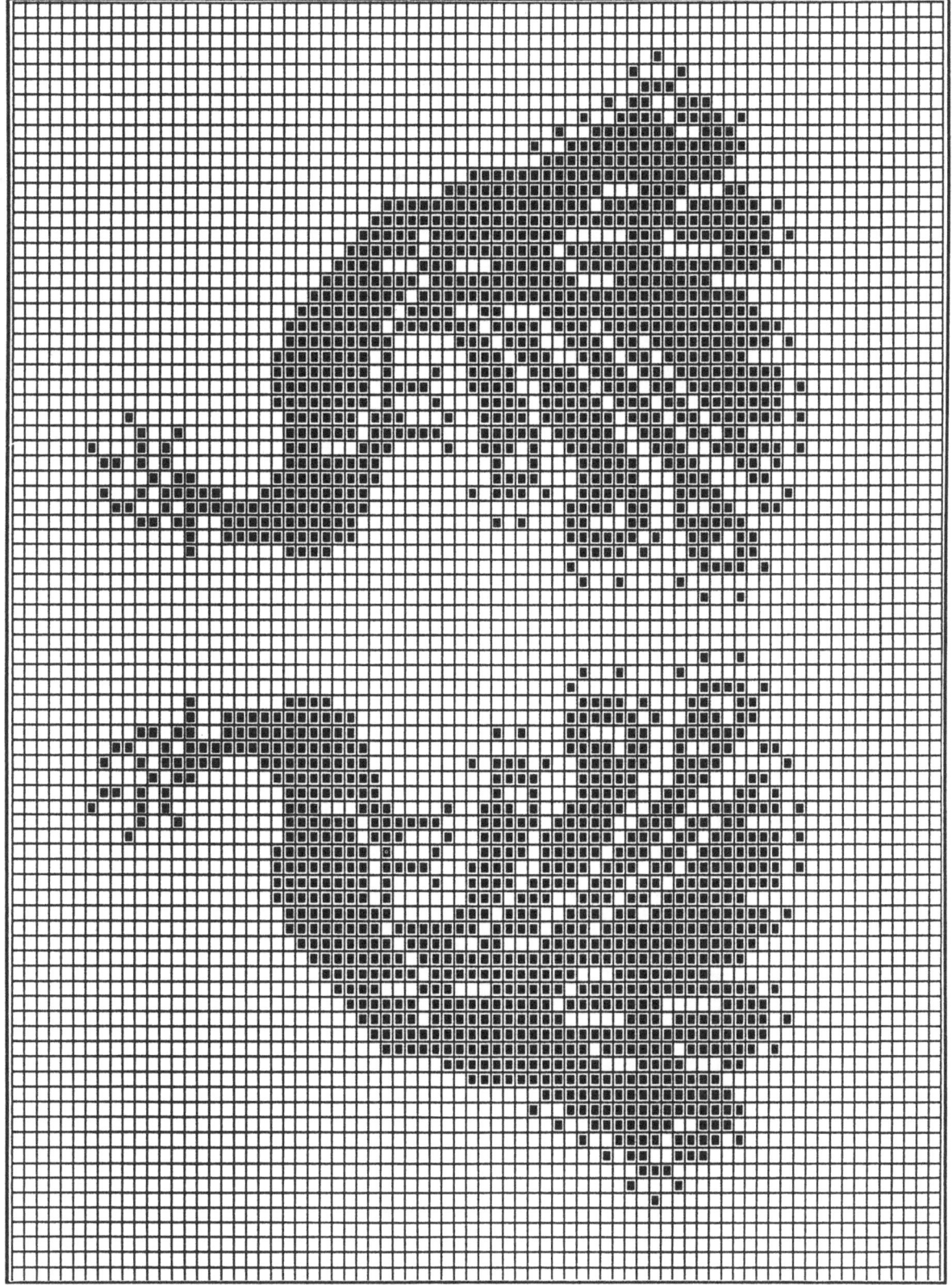

THE PEACOCK PATTERN WAS ON A SWEATER PURCHASED IN THE LATE 1930S. SUCH AN ELABORATE DESIGN IS FEASIBLE ONLY IN YARNS WHICH ALLOW THE USE OF LARGE NUMBERS OF STITCHES.

THE RAVEN, ABOVE, AND THE BEAVER, BELOW, ARE THE ONLY TWO DESIGNS FOUND TO INCORPORATE A THIRD COLOR. THESE DESIGNS ARE USUALLY WORKED IN BLACK ON A GRAY GROUND WITH WHITE AS THE THIRD COLOR (DESIGNATED BY X). THESE DESIGNS APPEAR TO HAVE BEEN INSPIRED BY THE CARVINGS OF THE NORTHWEST COAST INDIANS.

Chapter Eight
Notes for the Knitter

Before one of these wonderful Indian-inspired sweaters can be created, sufficient yarns of the proper diameter must be at hand. Yardage is critical, especially if using handspun yarn. If all the yarn of a particular carded blend has been used up, there is *no more* of that lot!

Experience is the best guide when estimating quantities. There is no way to accurately establish the yardage requirement for each individual sweater. These sweaters are made of handspun yarn and the yarn diameter varies from spinner to spinner. Furthermore, the gauge at which knitters work will vary. As a general reference for yardage requirements, a two-color sweater will require the amounts shown at right. The actual yardage will depend upon the yarn, the designs selected, needle size and how firmly the yarn is tensioned on the needles. These suggested yardages are strictly for reference.

Yarn

Yardage Needed

SIZE	MAIN COLOR	CONTRAST COLOR
Child to XS	500-650 yards	150-200 yards
Small	650-850 yards	250-300 yards
Medium	850-1000 yards	300-350 yards
Large-XL	1000-1200 yards	350-400 yards

Sizing Systems

Each Salish knitter has a formula for knitting a sweater – her own personal standard pattern. Although all the formulas are based on body proportions, no two knitters' formulas are identical. In this book, in order to simplify sizing, all of the critical measurements have been converted to a percentage system. (See chart and diagrams on next page.) This system is based on the chest measurement plus the ease stitches equalling 100%. All other measurements are a portion thereof. The various proportions, expressed as percentages, are shown in the chart, along with the numbers from the hypothetical example below.

To clarify the use of a percentage system, in the following example the knitter has worked up a swatch and determined that the gauge is 3 stitches and 4 rows to the inch. The sweater is to fit an individual with a chest measurement of 34 inches. It will be a pullover in two colors, so 650-850 yards of the main color and 250-300 yards of the contrast color are necessary. (See yardage chart.)

In this example, there are 120 stitches in the circumference to work design repeats. If a design repeat is 6 or 10 stitches, it works out

Calculating Sizing Percentages for a Salish Sweater

Body

GAUGE: 3 STITCHES/INCH; 4 ROWS/INCH

CHEST MEASUREMENT + EASE = 100%
    100% = 34" + 6" = 40"
    40" X 3 STITCHES / INCH = 120 STITCHES

HIPBAND = 90% = .9 X 40" = 36"
    36" X 3 STITCHES / INCH = 108 STITCHES
    A 2 X 2 RIBBING HAS A REPEAT OF 4: 108/4 = 27
    A 2 X 1 RIBBING HAS A REPEAT OF 3: 108/3 = 36

DEPTH TO UNDERARM = 40% = .4 X 40" = 16"
    16" X 4 ROWS/INCH = 64 ROWS

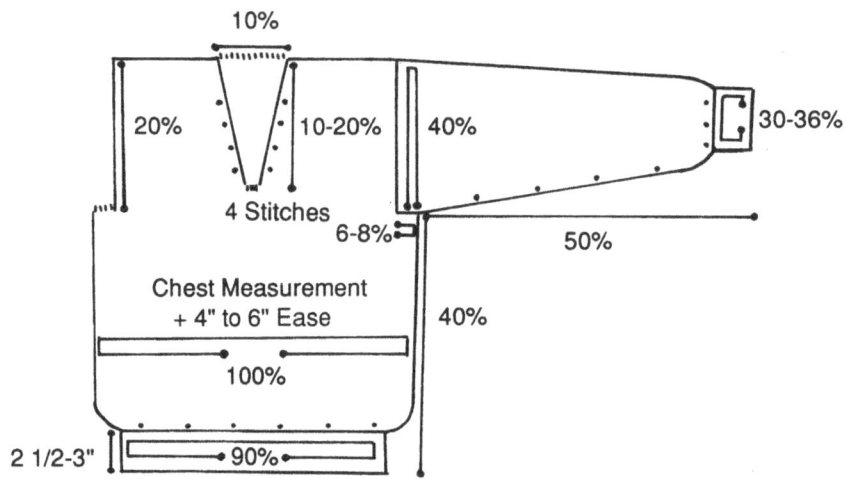

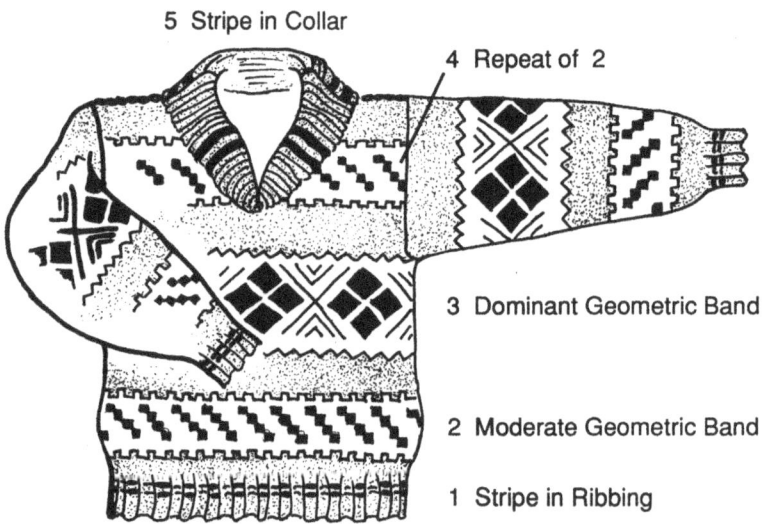

ABOVE: BASIC PULLOVER WITH FORMULAS
BELOW: PULLOVER REPRESENTING CLASSIC DESIGN FORMULA WITH FIVE PATTERN BANDS ON HEATHERED GROUND

Neck

BACK NECK = 10% = .1 X 40" = 4"
  4" X 3 STITCHES / INCH = 12 STITCHES

FRONT NECK DEPTH :
- HIGH NECK = 10% =.1 X 40" = 4"
  4" X 4 ROWS / INCH = 16 ROWS
- DEEP V-NECK = 20% = .2 X 40" = 8"
  8" X 4 ROWS / INCH = 32 ROWS
  (FROM 32 ROWS TO 15 ROWS, DEPENDING ON PREFERENCE)

V-NECK DECREASES =
  BACK NECK STITCHES - 4 STITCHES FOR FRONT COLLAR BASE
  12 STITCHES - 4 STITCHES = 8 DECREASES:
  PLACE 4 DECREASES ON EACH SIDE.

Sleeves

SLEEVE CAP = 40% = .4 X 40" = 16"
  16" X 3 STITCHES / INCH = 48 STITCHES

SLEEVE CIRCUMFERENCE = SLEEVE CAP + UNDERARM
  48 STITCHES + 10 STITCHES = 58 STITCHES

SLEEVE LENGTH = 50% = .5 X 40" = 20"
  20" X 4 ROWS / INCH = 80 ROWS

CUFF = 30% - 36%
  30% = .3 X 40" = 12"
  12" X 3 STITCHES / INCH = 36 STITCHES
  36% = .36 X 40" = 14.4"
  14.4" X 3 STITCHES / INCH = 43.2"
  (ADJUST TO 44 FOR K2, P2 RIB)

SLEEVE DECREASES = SLEEVE CIRCUMFERENCE - CUFF
  58 STITCHES - 40 STITCHES = 18 DECREASES
  PLACE HALF DOWN SLEEVE LENGTH, HALF AT CUFF: 5 PAIRED DECREASES DOWN LENGTH,
  8 DECREASES AT CUFF.

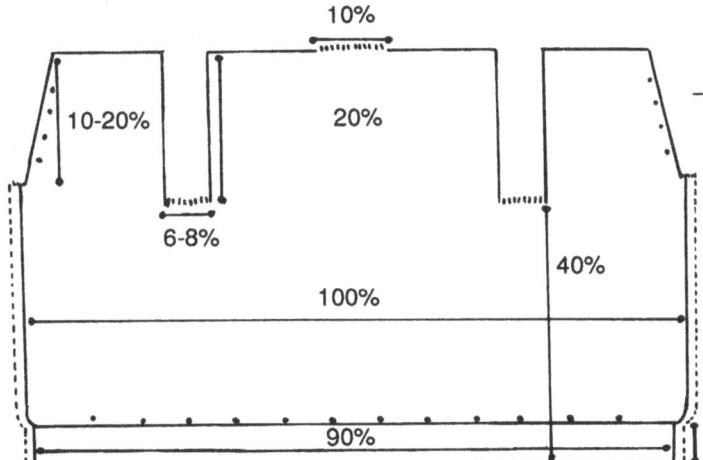

2 Stitches for Zipper
6 Stitches for Buttons

2 1/2-3"

No Stripes in Collar
Large complimentary Geometric Band
3 Repeat of 1
2 Representational Design Replacing Dominant Geometric Band
1 Moderate Geometric Band
No stripes in Ribbing

ABOVE: BASIC CARDIGAN WITH FORMULAS.
BELOW: MODERN CARDIGAN IN TWO COLORS WITH THREE BANDS OF DESIGN.

NOTES FOR THE KNITTER

evenly. If the design repeat is 9 stitches, the knitter needs to alter the total number of stitches. As 6 inches of ease was allowed, the total circumference stitches could be changed to 117 for a 9-stitch repeat. Vertically, there are 94 rows in the body of the sweater. Subtracting 10 rows for the hipband ribbing leaves 84 rows in which to place the bands of pattern.

The Salish System

Salish knitters do *not* use the percentage system described above. It is presented as a guide for the typical proportions followed on an "average" Indian sweater of this style. The Salish patterns are based on the chest-plus-ease figure for the circumference. Standard stitch counts are then followed for the various areas of the sweater. The stitch counts for each area of the sweater and for each size are listed in the *Typical Stitch Counts* chart below.

All sweater lengths are based on actual measurements taken for custom work. For general sweater construction, proportion is determined rather casually. The length to underarm is "almost as long as the body is wide." The armhole depth is "less than half as wide as the body." The V opening for the collar is "not quite as deep as the armhole," because that makes a nice-sized collar "without it getting too big." The sleeve is "about as long as the body is wide." This might sound like an offhand way to approach sizing, but, as a rule, it works. These knitters know that there is considerable latitude in what will and will not fit when it comes to knitwear!

Typical Stitch Counts

SIZE (CHEST MEAS.)	UNDERARM STITCHES	COLLAR BASE CENTER FRONT	DECREASES AT FRONT NECK	COLLAR BASE BACK NECK	DECREASES ON SLEEVE
CHILD TO XS (UP TO 30")	4-6	ALL SIZES: 2-4 FOR PULLOVER; 2 EACH SIDE FOR ZIPPERED CARDIGAN; 6 EACH SIDE FOR BUTTONED CARDIGAN (CHILD'S MAY HAVE ONLY 5)	2	8	2-3 PAIRED
SMALL (32 - 34")	8-10		3	10	3-4 PAIRED
MEDIUM (36"- 38")	10-12		4	12	4-5 PAIRED
LARGE TO XL (40" AND UP)	12-14		5	14	4-5 PAIRED

Careful Planning

For most knitters, calculating the total number of stitches and rows in the entire garment is important. The designs selected must fit into the given amount of space. The actual number of stitches and rows can be altered to accomodate various designs, but adjustments are limited with these bulky yarns. In some cases, alternative designs might be necessary. Until sufficiently experienced to "know", as is the case of the Salish knitter, there is no substitute for careful planning.

Stitch Proportions

It is important to note the proportion of the knit stitch to the purl stitch in planning a sweater. There are always more rows than knit stitches per square inch for any given area. This is important when calculating the number of stitches in the sleeve cap as compared to the number of rows in the armhole. Sleeve cap stitches are not picked up at the end of every row. In most cases, skipping every fifth row is successful, but since there is a limited number of stitches in the bulky Salish sweater, calculating the actual number according to one's guage is recommended.

Decrease Option

In the sweaters studied, Salish knitters used the standard Sl1, K1, PSSO for the left-leaning decrease. Using the SSK decrease produces a smoother left-slant than the stair-step effect of the PSSO decrease. The recommended SSK decrease option is illustrated below.

INSTRUCTIONS: *SSK Decrease*

- Slip the first stitch knitwise to twist the loop.
- Slip a second stitch in the same manner.
- Bring left needle tip through on the front side of the 2 slipped stitches, and knit both off together.

SSK DECREASE

A. TWO STITCHES SLIPPED KNITWISE.

B. BOTH SLIPPED STITCHES REPOSITIONED AND KNIT TOGETHER.

C. FINAL APPEARANCE

Modified Intarsia Option

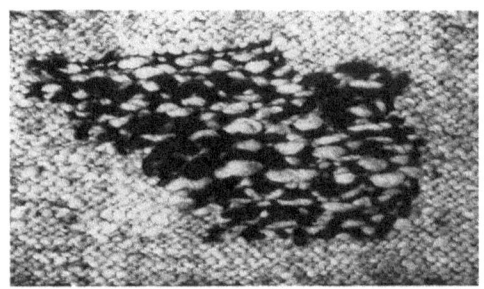

DETAIL, MODIFIED INTARSIA TECHNIQUE. PATTERN COLOR IS NOT CARRIED BEYOND THE DESIGN.

When working a pattern motif, the Salish knitter traditionally weaves the stranding yarn onto the back when a color is not in use. See photo, page 74. This practice eliminates long floats which can be easily snagged in use. Woven stranding is very effective in the geometric bands, but the use of the modified intarsia technique as practised by a few of the Indian knitters today is recommended for representational motifs. With this technique the pattern color does not have to be carried for long distances, but is used only within the design area. The background color is typically used within the design area. It is carried throughout and woven onto the back when not in use. This modified form of intarsia uses less of the pattern yarn and can significantly reduce the weight of the finished garment. Intarsia techniques can only be worked back and forth, however, limiting their use to cardigan styles.

Zippers for Salish Cardigans

Heavy-duty separating zippers for jackets are available at most fabric stores. They range in length from 12" to 36," sized at two-inch intervals. Medium-weight separating zippers as small as 8" can be found for infant and small child's cardigans. Zippers in the commercially-produced Salish sweaters typically have brass teeth on twill tape, and are available in tan, brown, gray and black. In addition to the traditional brass, YKK™ produces a heavy-duty parka zipper in a man-made material that is of excellent quality. These come in grays to black and tans to brown, plus white and off-white. Both teeth and fabric tape match in color.

As the zippers are commercially produced in even lengths, it is wise to plan in advance for the starting point of the collar. If necessary, the zipper can extend under the collar for a short distance. Should an odd length be required, some upholsterers will cut zippers to length.

To attach the zipper, back-stitching by hand with button-heavy craft thread is recommended. This allows for an easy replacement without damaging the sweater should the zipper wear out after several seasons of use. The average home sewing machine will not accomodate stitching on this type of garment, so if machine-stitching is desired, check with an upholsterer.

Many of the Salish knitting techniques should not be limited to use on Indian-style sweaters. For example, the double bind-off shoulder join, whereby the front and back stitches are bound off simultaneously, (p.58) is an elegant treatment for most sweaters. In a sweater made with fine yarns, working the bind-off with a double strand results in a decorative braid on the shoulders. The half-gusset at the underarm (p. 70) gives a superior fit, even to a high-fashion sweater. This is especially true when the half-gusset is combined with a shaped armhole (p. 54) and shaped sleeve cap (p. 71). Mastering the craft of knitting is often most successful if the old ways – folk traditions – are integrated into everyday knitting!

Applying Salish Techniques

A FULL-FASHION SWEATER UTILIZING SALISH KNITTING TECHNIQUES. MADE OF 100% ALPACA YARN ON SIZE ONE NEEDLES, IT WAS KNIT IN THE ROUND TO THE UNDERARMS. UNDERARM STITCHES WERE SET ASIDE; FRONT AND BACK WORKED SEPARATELY. THE ARMHOLES WERE SHAPED. THE SHOULDERS WERE SHAPED WITH SHORT ROWS (NOT IN THE SALISH MANNER), THEN BOUND OFF SIMULTANEOUSLY WITH A DOUBLE STRAND OF YARN TO CREATE A BRAID EFFECT. THE SLEEVES WERE PICKED UP AND WORKED DOWN, A SLEEVE CAP SHAPED BY WORKING BACK AND FORTH TO THE CURVED SECTION OF THE UNDERARM. A HALF-GUSSET WAS DEVELOPED ON THE UNDERSIDE OF THE SLEEVE THEN THE SLEEVE WAS CONTINUED TO THE CUFF.

NOTES FOR THE KNITTER

RIGHT: CLOSE-UP OF SHOULDER AND UPPER SLEEVE. NOTE THE HALF-GUSSET AT THE UNDERARM, SHAPED CAP AND SHOULDER JOIN. THE CAP WAS BUILT OVER THE ENTIRE STRAIGHT AREA OF THE ARMHOLE, JOINING AND WORKING IN THE ROUND WHEN THE CURVED SECTION COMMENCES. THEREAFTER THE HALF-GUSSET IS DEVELOPED AT BOTH THE FRONT AND BACK OF THE UNDERARM STITCHES.

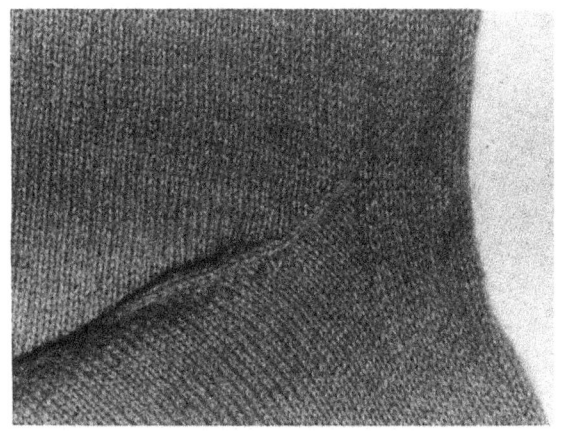

DETAIL OF HALF-GUSSET AT UNDERARM. THE VERTICAL SECTIONS IS THE UNDERARM STITCHES. THE HALF-GUSSET LIES AS A SMALL TRIANGLE BETWEEN THE UNDERARM STITCHES AND THE CURVE OF THE SHAPED ARMHOLE.

BELOW RIGHT: DETAIL OF SHOULDERS JOINED WITH SALISH DOUBLE BIND-OFF. SHOULDERS WERE SHAPED WITH SHORT ROWS. THE SHORT ROWS WERE JOINED INTO THE ROW ABOVE AS THEY WERE WORKED IN STOCKINETTE STITCH. AT THE TOP OF THE ARMHOLE, THE SAME NUMBER OF STITCHES WAS PICKED UP AS IN THE UNDERARM. A CAP WAS THEN WORKED BACK AND FORTH, ADDING NEW STITCHES AT EACH END TO GRADUALLY BUILD THE SHAPING.

BIBLIOGRAPHY

ASHWELL, REG. *Coast Salish: Their Art, Culture & Legends.* Surrey: Hancock House, 1978.

BARNETT, H.G. *The Coast Salish of British Columbia.* Eugene: University of Oregon Press, 1955.

BROTHERS, RYAN. "Cowichan Knitters," in *The Beaver* (Summer, 1965), pp 42-46.

*BUXTON-KEENLYSIDE, JUDITH. *Selected Canadian Spinning Wheels in Perspective: An Analytical Approach.* Ottawa: National Museum of Man, 1980 (Mercury Series).

COMPTON, RAE. *The Complete Book of Traditional Knitting.* New York: Charles Scribner's Sons, 1983.

DON, SARAH. *Fair Isle Knitting.* London: Mills & Boon, Ltd., 1979.

GIBSON-ROBERTS, PRISCILLA A. *Knitting in the Old Way.* Loveland, Colorado: Interweave Press, 1985.

GIBSON-ROBERTS, PRISCILLA A. "Big and Bold –The Cowichan Style," in *Knitters*, Issue 5, Fall/Winter 1986), pp 61-65.

*GUSTAFSON, PAULA. *Salish Weaving.* Seattle: University of Washington Press, 1980.

HARRINGTON, LYN. "The Cowichan Sweater," in *Canadian Geographic Journal*, Vol. XXXX, No. 2 (February 1950).

HAWKINS, ELIZABETH. *Iindian Weaving, Knitting & Basketry of the Northwest.* Vancouver: Hancock House, 1978.

HOBBS, ANNA. "Cowichan Indian Sweaters: The Warm, Wonderful Status Symbol," in *Canadian Living*, Vol. 4, No. 9 (September, 1979), pp 40-45.

HOBBS, ANNA. "Weaving a History," in *Canadian Living*, Vol. II, No.9 (September 1986), pp 106-111.

JOHNSON, ELIZABETH & BERNICK, KATHRYN. *Hands of Our Ancestors: The Revival of Salish Weaving at Musqueam.* Vancouver: U.B.C. Museum of Anthropology, 1986. (Museum Note No. 16.)

*KISSELL, MARY LOIS. "A New Type of Spinning in North America," in *American Anthropologist*, VOL. 18 (1916), pp 264-270.

*LANE, BARBARA. "The Cowichan Knitting Industry," in *Anthropology in British Columbia.* Victoria: British Columbia Provincial Museum, Vol. 2 (1951), pp 14-27.

MARR, CAROLYN J. *A History of Salish Weaving: The Effects of Culture Change on a Textile Tradition.* Colorado: Unversity of Denver, 1979. Unpublished M.A. Thesis.

MCGREGOR, SHEILA. *The Complete Book of Traditional Fair Isle Knitting.* New York: Charles Scribner's Sons, 1982.

*MCGREGOR, SHEILA. *Traditional Knitting.* London: Batsford, 1983.

*MEIKLE, MARGARET. *Cowichan Indian Knitting.* Vancouver: U.B.C. Museum of Anthropology, 1987. (Museum Note No. 21).

MEIKLE, MARGARET. "The Cowichan Knitting Industry." Unpublished paper presented to the Native American Art Studies Association, September 1983.

MEIKLE, MARGARET. "The Cowichan Band." in *Knitters*, Issue 5, (Fall/Winter, 1985). p. 60

NORCROSS, E. BLANCHE. "The Cowichan Sweater," in *The Beaver.* (December, 1945) pp. 18-19.

PEARSON, MICHAEL. *Traditional Knitting: Aran, Fair Isle & Fisher Gansey.* New York: Van Nostrand Reinhold, 1984.

RUTT, RICHARD. *A History of Knitting.* London: Batsford, 1987.

*STARMORE, ALICE. *Alice Starmore's Book of Fair Isle Knitting.* Newtown, Connecticut: The Taunton Press, 1988.

*STELZER, ULLI. *Indian Artists At Work.* Seattle: University of Washington Press, 1976.

WELLS, OLIVER N. *Salish Weaving: Primitive and Modern.* Sardis, B.C.: Oliver N. Wells, 1969.

WELLS, OLIVER N. *The Chilliwacks and Their Neighbors.* Vancouver: Talonbooks, 1987.

ZIMMERMANN, ELIZABETH. *Knitting Workshop.* Pittsville, Wisconsin: Schoolhouse Press, 1981.

INDEX

Armholes, 54, 55, 71, 109

Bands, 5
   Cowichan, 5
   Musqueam, 5
   Chilliwack, 5
Basket Making, 6, 73
Basketry Designs, 21
Batt, 34, 37, 42
Beaver Motif, 26, 28
Bias Twist, 43
Bibliography, 115
Bind-Off Sleeve Join, 68
Bind-off Together
   Shoulder Join, 18, 57, 113
Blanket, Ceremonial, 10
Blanket, Common Salish,
   6, 10, 11, 24
Blanket, Early, 8
Blanket, Goat Hair, 5, 6, 10
British Columbia Provincial
   Museum, 16, 18, 27, 38
British Columbia Native
   Craft Show, 31
Bulk-Head Spinner, 38, 39

Cape Flattery, 6
Cardigan, 22, 47, 78, 109, 112
   Cut, 22, 47
   Edgings for, 47
   Knit As, 22, 29
   Raw Edges On, 22, 47
   Zippers In, 22, 29, 112
Carder, Drum, 26, 36, 37, 42
Carder, Hand, 35, 36
Carding, 35
   Custom, 27, 31, 37
Charles, Christine, 19
Charles, Clara, 72, 74
Charlie, Mrs. Pat, 22
Charts, 81-106
Chilliwack Museum, 30
Coast Salish, 5, 10, 21
Collars. See Shawl Collars
Color-Stranded Patterns,
   16, 17, 18, 46, 73
   Color-Standing Techniques,
   18, 46, 73, 74, 76
Colvin, Jermina, 16,18, 21
Combing, 42
Cottage Industry, 15, 21, 24, 31
Cowichan, 3, 19
   Band, 1, 3, 5, 15, 18, 26
   Historical Museum, 18
   Knitters, 18, 19, 21
   Sweaters, 5, 18, 19, 22
   Valley, 13
Crimp, 34, 41

Design Bands, 19, 78
Design, Sources, 75
Designs, 18, 19
   Early, 25
   Geometric, 45, 73, 75,
      84-107
   In Childrens sweaters, 78
   Placement, 77, 78, 108, 109
   Recorded In Samplers,
      26, 76, 77
   Representational,
      26, 45, 74, 75, 76, 78,
      88-106
   Sharing Of, 26, 77, 79

Dog Hair, 7
Double Bind-Off
   Shoulder Join, 58, 59
      Four-Needles, 59
      Three Needles, 59
Draw, 42, 43
Duncan B.C., 1, 32
   Fall Fair, 28
Dyes, 35, 74

Ease, 49, 107, 108
Edging. See Cardigan

Fair Isle Jersey, 17, 18, 19
Fair Isle Knitting, 1
Fibers, 7, 31
   Blending, 15, 42, 36, 37
   Preparation, 8, 35, 42
   Fleece, 33, 39, 41
Ft. Langley, 11
Ft. Vancouver, 11
Ft. Victoria, 13
Fraser River, 5, 7
Full-Fashion Sweater, 113, 114

Gansey, British Fisherman's,
   16, 17, 18, 19
Gee, Mary Sue, 24
George, Nora,
   8, 20, 25, 45, 61, 70, 75
Great Britain, 13
Grafted Shoulder Join, 18
Grafted Sleeve Join, 69
Grafting, Underarm
   Stitches, 69
Guerin, Martha, 20
Gussets, 17, 71
Handspindle, 6
Heathered Yarn,
   19, 42, 74, 78
Hudson's Bay Company,
   11, 13, 31
Hudson's Bay Blanket, 12

Indian Head Spinner, 38, 42
Indian Sweater, 15, 16, 18
Interior Salish, 5

Joe, Monica, 20, 28, 71

Kelly, Josephine, 30, 36
Knit In The Round, 14, 17, 19
Knitting, Circular, 46
Knitting,ContinentalStyle,14
Knitting, Family
   Characteristics, 25
Knitting Instruction, 13
Knitting Techniques, 45
Koksilah Reserve, 3, 77
Kwakason, Chief George, 13

Loom, Salish, 9, 10

Map, 2
Mission Schools, 13
Mittens, 14
Modified Intarsia, 73, 105

Natural-Colored Wools,
   19, 45, 74
Neck Shaping,
   19, 54, 55, 56, 109
Northwest Coast Indians, 5

Olympic Peninsula, 5
OXO Pattern, 76, 77, 89

Page, Edith, 7, 27, 73, 77
Paige, Harriet, 78
Percentage System,
   107, 108, 109
Picking Up Stitches At
   Armhole, 67
Pocket Borders, 54
Pockets, Horizontal, 49
   Reinforcement, 50
Pockets, Slanted, 45, 51
   Slanted Liners, 53
   Vertical Liners, 52
Potlatch, 11, 12
Puget Sound, 5
Pullover, 16, 47, 55, 107
   Collars on, 66
Purl-Slipstitch Pattern, 23, 76

Representational Designs.
   See Designs
Rolag, 34
Rose Motif, 13
Roving, Commercial, 34
Royal British Columbia
   Museum, 6, 7, 13, 15, 20, 22

SSK Decrease, 111
Saanich Reserve, 18
Salish Blanket. See Blanket

Salish Indians, 3, 19, 21
   See also: Coast Salish,
      Interior Salish
Salish Knitting Tradition, 4
Salish Sweaters,
   5, 23, 28, 33, 45, 71, 73,
   108, 109
   Early, 16, 47
   Future of, 21, 23, 24, 27,
      29, 31
   Imitations, 23
   Inferior, 22, 23
   Labelling of, 23
   Quality in, 22, 23,, 27, 29
   Unique Aspects of, 21
Salish System For Sizing, 108
Salish Weaving, 6, 9, 10, 30
   Revival of, 31
Salish Wool, 34
Samplers, 26, 76, 77
Scotland, 13
Scottish Inspiration, 21
Shawl Collar, 5, 16, 18, 19,
   45, 61-66
   Alternate Shaping of, 64
   Continuous, 64
      Flare In Front, 65
      Flare In Back, 66
   Three-Unit, 18, 61
      Collar Back, 62
      Collar Back with
         Stand, 63
      Collar Fronts, 61
Shed, 9
Sheep, 13
Shetland Islands, 16, 19
Shoulder Joins, 57
Simmer Bath, 43
Sleeve Cap, 70

Sleeves, 66
   Joining To Body, 68, 69
   Worked Down,
      17, 29, 66, 67, 68
   Worked Up, 29, 66, 67, 68
Slip-Stitch Pattern.
   See Purl-Slipstitch
Socks, 14
Spindle, 6, 7, 8, 38, 41
Spindle Spinning, 14
Spindle Whorl, 8
Spinning, 6, 14
Spinning Machine, 14, 38
Spinning Wheel, 33
Spirit Dance, 11
Steek, 17, 46
Stitch Calculation, 110
Stitch Proprtions, 111
Sul' Sul' Tin, 8
Sweater Body, 49

Tension Ring, 7
Third Color, 26, 74, 75
Thorne, Agnes, 23
Toques, 14
Totem Pole Motif, 26
Trading Posts, 11
Triple Bind-Off, 60
Twill Weave, 10
Twine Weave, 10
Twist, 14, 39, 43
   Angle Of, 37
   Bias, 41
   S and Z, 14, 39, 43
   Setting, 37, 43
Two-Stitch Border, 46, 47, 48

Underwear, Knee Length, 15
University of British Columbia
   Museum of Anthropology,
   19, 27, 51, 62

V-Neck, 16, 45, 55, 109
Valdeez Island, 19
Vancouver Island,
   3, 5, 13, 15, 21, 31

Watson, Debbie, 66
Weaving Loom, 8
Weaving Frame, 8
Wells, Oliver, 31
West Coast Indian Motif, 26
White, Betty, 20, 21, 23,28, 71,
   72, 73, 75, 76, 77, 78
White Buffalo Yarn, 44
Williams, Eva, 49
Wool, 31, 32 See also: Fibers
   Preparation, 35
   Selection, 34
   Staple Length, 34
Woolen Yarn, 39
Worsted Yarn, 39
Woven Motifs, 9
Wraps Per Inch, 37

Yardage, 107
Yarn, 33, 37, 100
   Bulky , 14, 33, 34, 41
   Handspun Singles, 16, 33
   Heavy Weight, 14
   Suitable for Salish Knits, 41

Zippers. See Cardigans

www.ingramcontent.com/pod-product-compliance
Lightning Source LLC
Chambersburg PA
CBHW051551220426
43671CB00025B/2998